The
Fiction Writers'
Handbook

The Fiction Writers' Handbook

NANCY SMITH

PIATKUS

Dedication

To my children, Jan, Richard and Mark, for
their unfailing love and encouragement

Acknowledgement

My grateful thanks to Lewis Hosegood for permission to
reprint his story *Homesickness*.

Copyright © 1991 Nancy Smith

First published in 1991 by Judy Piatkus (Publishers) Ltd
5 Windmill Street, London W1P 1HF

Reprinted 1993

**The moral right of the author
has been asserted**

*A catalogue record for this book is available
from the British Library*

ISBN 0-7499-1047-X
ISBN 0-7499-1152-2 (Pbk)

Edited by Maggie Daykin
Designed by Sue Ryall

Set in Linotron Baskerville by
Computerset Ltd, Harmondsworth
Printed and bound in Great Britain by
Biddles Ltd, Guildford and King's Lynn

Contents

SECTION THREE *The short story*

SECTION FOUR *The practical side of writing*

SECTION FIVE *In brief*

Introduction

'There is no Frigate like a book,
To take us Lands away.'
Emily Dickinson

Emily Dickinson's poem says it all: whether we are reader or writer, we are transported to another world. Immersed in a novel or a short story, we can forget about any personal problems for a while, and escape into a fantasy-land, to emerge – one hopes – enriched, enlightened and uplifted.

But, as this book is about writing, have you considered why you want to write? Why do any of us want to? Is it because there is something we are bursting to say? Is it possibly also because it gives us a certain reassurance? We may not be in charge of our own destinies but we do control those of the characters we create. In that respect, we can play God.

Assuming there are plots and themes, ideas and characters all jostling round in your head, struggling to be put down on paper, that you are willing to draw upon your own experience and emotions, painful as well as pleasant, this book will help you to find the right vehicle for them – either short story or novel. It explains various techniques of fiction-writing, all of which every aspiring writer – however talented – needs to understand and employ. Some, perhaps the more gifted, the 'born' writers, may learn through prolific reading. Others (the majority of us) need initial guidance if we are to avoid the basic mistakes that lead to rejection, dejection and giving up forever.

Here, let me say what will be reiterated throughout the book: it is perseverance that ultimately brings success. Many would-be writers have fallen by the wayside, not because they lacked inherent talent but because they lacked the determination to persist. Perseverance is an important function of success.

The 'rules' set out in the following pages are merely tools that enable you, the writer, to transfer emotions and experiences on to paper. As with any other discipline, once you have learned to use them *effectively*, you can experiment – even break them – provided you do so purposefully. They are aids to writing, not cords to bind and stifle your creativity. But, remember, they have evolved through centuries of story-telling. Discard them only after reasoned thought.

In this book, I have tried to pass on to you everything that *I* have learned about fiction-writing, over the years – and we never *stop* learning. There is always a new way of looking at something, a fresh angle, an original twist to give to a worn plot. I have used, too, the methods I have found effective with those I have taught over a period of thirteen years; by using them many students having had the tremendous pleasure and excitement of seeing their stories in print, at last, sometimes after years of rejections. Often, all that was needed was a tiny beam, shedding light on one particular aspect they had found difficult or, perhaps, not fully understood – be it structure, the need to 'show' rather than 'tell' or to create believable characters instead of 'cardboard cutouts'.

What else does a writer need? A writer must have 'the common touch': must have an insatiable curiosity in people, places and events. In the words of John Donne, s/he must be 'involved in mankind'. S/he must also understand the differences between the short story and the novel (not simply a matter of length) and be familiar with the various ingredients. As with making a cake, all of these ingredients are interdependent.

Without believable, flesh-and-blood characters with whom readers can identify and empathise, the story isn't likely to interest him or her sufficiently to make them carry on reading till the end. This means ensuring they act and speak 'in character', which involves writing good, effective dialogue.

Without conflict, there is no story. Conflict is the rising agent, the yeast, in your bread. Excellent though everything else in it may be, if it doesn't rise it will be a flop.

Viewpoint is another vitally important aspect to consider before you start to write any story. Ask yourself: whose story is it? Should it be narrated in the first or third person, by one or more characters?

All of these ingredients, and more, need to be considered and the techniques involved understood. I hope this book will help you blend them into successful stories that will be published – and eagerly read.

The techniques of fiction-writing

In my Introduction, I suggested that one of the reasons we want to write fiction may be for reassurance. That, with fiction, we can create a world in which we are in control. I'd like to explore the idea a little more fully.

Dorothy Rowe in *Beyond Fear* says: 'In every moment of our experience, we are explaining our world to ourselves. This way, we *master* our experience.' Dorothy Rowe is an eminent psychologist – and psychology, surely, is the science of understanding ourselves and our emotions, other people and theirs? To become a writer of fiction, it is axiomatic that we have an insatiable curiosity about what makes people tick; we must become amateur psychologists, students of human nature.

SHORT STORY VERSUS NOVEL

So, now, what kind of fiction do you want to write? First, perhaps you should think about what kind you most like to read. Do you read short stories for pleasure? Though mostly to be found in women's magazines, these should not be despised; often, they are by well-known and respected writers and skilfully crafted. (Although, to a degree, we must accept that whatever an eminent writer produces will probably find its way into print.)

Do you enjoy anthologies of short stories, perhaps by one particular favourite author? Or by various new writers first published in collections? These include the now well-established annual Ian St. James Award, Heinemann's first new writing anthology (published 1990) with the delightful title *And God gives nuts to those who have no teeth*, and Yorkshire Art Circus's *Yorkshire Mixture* – supported by, among others, Yorkshire Arts. While established writers of the stature of Frank O'Connor, Sean O'Faolain, H.E. Bates, William Trevor and Penelope Lively, to name but a few, can teach us a good deal about the craft of the short story, the above mentioned publications – and others like them – offer encouragement to the rest of us.

If you *are* interested in the short story, there are definite advantages in starting your career with this form of fiction rather than the novel. For one thing, it doesn't take so long to write (though it doesn't follow that it is easier) and, therefore, isn't such a daunting task as tackling a full-length work of say, 80,000 plus words. It also provides an excellent means of serving your apprenticeship in learning the 'tricks of the trade'. For instance, how to produce effective dialogue, create sympathetic and/or interesting characters, build suspense and tension, write in scenes (the old 'show, don't tell' of which you will hear more, later in this book.)

Your chances of success will also be greatly increased because there are large numbers of magazines (not to mention BBC Radio 4) constantly seeking good-quality short fiction – but the emphasis is on quality. Indeed, if they were *not* seeking good new writers, I doubt so many would run short story competitions. And with success, even a tiny one, your self-confidence in your ability as a writer will begin to grow. You can tell yourself: 'I've done it once, I can do it again!'

Lastly, once you have mastered the discipline of the short story with its infinitely tighter structure, you will find the novel less intimidating to attempt.

WRITING FOR MONEY OR LOVE?

At this point, we might consider another reason for putting pen to paper, or black on white, as Maupassant said. Is it for love of writing or money – or both? It is important to ponder on this because, depending upon your answer, I suspect, hinges how much effort you are prepared to put into it. After all, would you bother to train as, say, a doctor, a musician, a train-driver, a teacher; would you bother to go to work at all if you were not paid for your labour? I doubt it. And writing *is* work – demanding work – both physically and emotionally. Dr Johnson's words, 'No man but a blockhead ever wrote, except for money', have become famous in the annals of literature. I think he meant that writing was so arduous that anyone would have to be stupid to do it for no reward.

Also, surely we write in order to communicate? And, if no one reads what we write then it is pointless, except as some kind of self-therapy. If it *is* for therapeutic reasons, *how* we express ourselves is of secondary importance, the same effect being achieved however we write. So, the chances are we won't try to improve the way we string the words together.

However, Somerset Maugham once said that: 'A book is incomplete until it has a reader', and André Maurois that: 'If his (a writer's) purpose is to express himself, ought it not to be enough for him that he should succeed in doing so? Is a cloud of witnesses really essential?' He then answers his own question: 'He, the writer, has written with the deliberate purpose of revealing the truth about himself and about the world as he sees it. The revelation can have no point unless it reaches those for whom it is intended.'

Finally, I would suggest that many people will only take our writing seriously when they discover that we are being paid for it and, being human, that is usually very important to us. In the last analysis, fairly or unfairly, the only criterion by which our work is judged is: is someone willing to hand over good money to read it?

3

CAN WRITING BE TAUGHT?

Before we get on to the actual techniques of fiction-writing, I want briefly to address the age-old question – can writing be taught? I firmly believe that, if someone has an inherent talent, then he/she can be taught the techniques that will bring that talent to fruition. In the US, creative writing courses are held at many universities. In the UK, creative writing is on the curriculum of East Anglia and Lancaster universities, and has produced writers of the calibre of Kazuo Ishiguro (1989 Booker Prize winner) and Rose Tremain (a runner-up for this prestigious prize). She, along with Malcolm Bradbury, is now a tutor at East Anglia. John Steinbeck, too, once sat in a creative writing class in the US.

So, if you have joined a class or are reading this book in the belief that writing is a subject that can be learned, you are in good company. And I say, in all humility, that writers never stop learning. What a good teacher can do is guide you on to the right path, help you find, and use correctly, the best tools for the job. Then it is up to you to practise regularly and to persevere, which is the only sure way of achieving success in any field.

CHARACTERISATION

Characters do make your story so let's look at ways in which to create believable ones and not cardboard cut-outs.

I said earlier that writers of fiction need to become students of human nature, with an insatiable curiosity about what makes people tick. This is not mere 'nosiness'; it is wanting to know *why* they behave in a particular way, what motivates them to take such and such an action. Somerset Maugham listed certain traits that a novelist must have:

- Creativeness
- Quickness of perception
- An attentive eye
- Power to profit by experience
- An absorbed interest in human nature.

We observe a friend, neighbour, acquaintance, acting in an apparently uncharacteristic way, and we ask – why? We hear or read of someone perpetrating some terrible deed. Writers, after the initial horror has subsided, ask – why? If we show no interest at all in what lay behind that act, then it is unlikely we will ever become writers.

Motivation

This is where we should consider motivation. Because unless you know what motivates your characters, determines what they do to try to solve their particular problem(s) or achieve their goal(s), the plot of your story (long or short) won't hold up, your characters' actions won't be believable. It is motivation that sets the story in motion and carries it through to the end.

Motivation, motion, emotion – all stem from the Latin *movere*, to move. Therefore, before we consider any other fictional technique, it makes sense to look first at this.

We read in the newspaper of a frightful murder, perhaps committed by someone who previously appeared to be perfectly sane, normal, respectable. After the first shock, we ask – why? What possible motivation was there? For the *writer*, the reason for the deed, the *motivation*, will go on niggling him or her until s/he brings his or her imagination to bear on the whole tragic episode. It isn't enough to say, for instance, that the man who pulled out a gun and slaughtered several innocent people was mad. He probably was, in the sense that his mind was unhinged at that particular moment. But what was the final straw that tipped him over the edge? The facts of the incident may be known to all through the media but, if a writer wishes to create a piece of fiction from it, he has to *imagine* what motivated this man to act in the way he did, build a logical sequence of events (backwards and forwards, as s/he sees fit) to explain the apparently inexplicable. Real life events, all too frequently, are anything but logical; fiction *must* be.

And, here, I will give a warning. Never try to write up a true-life incident *exactly as it happened* and present it as a piece of fiction. It never works – and it could lead to a lawsuit! Use the actual *incident* as a base upon which to build a story, yes – but that is all. As Henry James remarked: 'Life is all inclusion and confusion. Art is all discrimination and selection.'

Somerset Maugham's short story, *The Kite*, is an interesting example of believable motivation in operation. For those who don't know it, it is about a young man who used to spend an unhealthy amount of time with his parents and who then got married. The marriage wasn't successful and he became obsessed with kite-flying, a hobby he enjoyed with his parents. At last, his wife, driven beyond endurance, destroyed his most prized possession, his new kite. The story ends when he leaves her and goes to prison rather than maintain the wife he now hates. Another writer might well have imagined him murdering his wife in a fit of rage or given it a contrived 'happy ending', with each forgiving the other.

Obviously, this is where motivation and characterisation are symbiotically linked. The reader must be shown the Main Character's obsession growing so that, when the climax arrives (the blackest moment in the protagonist's story), his reaction is totally convincing. In *The Kite*, the young man gives up all pretence at being a 'normal' husband and reverts to what he really was all along – a little boy who doesn't want to grow up and assume responsibilities, preferring to desert his wife and go back to his mother and father.

Artistic truth is not the same as actual truth. (Indeed, as Picasso said: 'Art is a lie that tells us the truth'.) As a writer of fiction (or as a painter or poet, for that matter), you are living in a world that, in fact, does not exist while, at the same time, exploring an inner world that is very real in your own head. As Anaïs Nin suggested, we write to create a world we can live in. Henry James, when he said that a writer has the '. . . power to guess the unseen from the seen, to trace the implication of things . . .', was also stressing that the writer must know what motivates his characters, if what they do is to be believable.

There is another truism, which is that part of one's self goes into every character one creates. I think this is unavoidable – just as it is unavoidable not to model characters, at least in part, on people we have known. Georges Simenon said that 'Every writer tries to find himself through his characters.'

Let's consider, now, the process we go through when creating the chief characters in a story. (Although, from the moment we begin, we will probably know their sex, their age and the sort of background they come from because character and situation are inextricably linked at the moment of conception.)

MAIN CHARACTERS

Choosing names

Giving your characters suitable names is the first step in bringing them to life. Frequently, names have certain connotations in our minds. They also go in fashions, so that calling someone, say, Gladys, suggests a woman at least in her sixties. Edith will be 70-plus and so will Harold, George and Archibald. Wayne, Sharon, Debbie, on the other hand, will be of a much younger generation. These will also be from a particular social background, hardly likely to be the same as that of a Lavinia, Georgina and Charles.

It's unfortunate if you happen to associate the names John, Richard or David with an unpleasant person because, for most of us, I think they conjure up a picture of someone who is likeable, honest and dependable. In contrast, Adrian or Clive suggest, to me, someone less reliable, a bit of a 'smoothie', perhaps.

Choosing the right names for your characters is very important, not only to convey, immediately, something about them to the reader but also to make them 'live' in your own mind. Most fiction writers will tell you that their stories do not 'jell' until they feel happy with the names for their main characters, so it is wise to take time and trouble over them. Surnames, too, must fit – for the same reasons, James Fortescue is likely to be a quite different person from James Arkbuckle, isn't he? And Victoria Betteson-Smythe, surely, is from a completely different background to Vicky Jones? The former would *never* allow herself to be called Vicky, would she?

A word of warning, here: avoid having two or more names beginning with the same initial or sounding too similar as characters in the same story as it can be confusing for the reader. For example, Averil and Alison; Martin and Matthew; John and James; Melvyn and Mervyn.

Age and characteristics

You then need to decide when they were born. Their exact age may well be determined by events in your story so it is advisable to know precisely how old they are, rather than merely state they are 'middle-aged' or 'in their twenties'. If you're interested in astrology, you might find it useful to give them exact birth-dates and the reputed characteristics of their astrological signs. For example, Scorpios are notoriously secretive (not to mention sexy!); Cancerians are home-loving, sensitive and avid collectors; while Leos love the lime-light, can be bossy but have a generous streak. A neat little trick to help you get to know them better.

Family/Background

Next, what is their background, their socio-economic group? This is important because it will dictate how they dress, behave, speak, what sort of job they have, what ambitions they may have, where they live and so on. They may, of course, be struggling to forget their background and so will not act like the rest of their family or childhood friends. In this case, their speech, dress and behaviour may be exaggerated so that, instead of blending into their new social class, as they hope, they will stick out 'like a sore thumb'. This, too, will add depth to your characterisation.

You will see, then, why observation is so important, and why it is usually advisable to write about what you know. For example, to try to create an Irish navvy, a Polish refugee or an elderly Jewish matriarch when you have never even met such people, is likely to result in an unconvincing character;

or perhaps, even worse, create a totally unexpected effect. I remember, many years ago when I had just started to write, I joined a writers' circle and someone read out a manuscript that had us all falling about laughing. It was about the aristocracy, involving a Jeeves-type butler and other carica-tures of the type created by P.G. Wodehouse. It was all so over-the-top, written by someone who had no intimate knowledge of the background being depicted, that none of us took it seriously: we thought it was meant to be a spoof. Unfortunately, it eventually became clear that it was not intended to be funny. Its writer took umbrage, never came again and, presumably, never learned that vital first lesson we all must – to write about what we know.

Clothes and style

If someone dresses in clothes that are years out of date, it could indicate a disregard for fashion or that they are so short of money they have to haunt charity shops or jumble sales to buy them secondhand. If trousers have a knife-edge crease, their wearer is probably particular about his ap-pearance. If colours clash, that could suggest poor taste. If someone consistently chooses brilliant colours, that indi-cates they like to be noticed; someone of a more reserved nature, who prefers to blend into the background, will probably choose subdued tones. If a young woman wears an ankle-length Indian cotton dress, brightly-coloured beads, is bare-footed or shod in flat sandals and has long, perhaps unruly, hair, we know she is somewhat unconventional.

The way they talk is obviously another very important way in which to bring your characters to life. Dialogue has a section to itself, later, so here, suffice to say that, in the words of A.E. Coppard, 'A character doesn't come alive until he speaks.'

Mannerisms/Behaviour

Body language, behaviour and mannerisms, all give vital clues to the character we are building.

If a woman straightens a picture on the wall, plumps up cushions and jumps up to wipe away even a tiny drop of spilled liquid, we know, without being told, she is overly house-proud. If a man brushes an imaginary speck of fluff off his suit sleeve, smoothes his hair and glances at himself in the mirror before going out, we can be sure he is very conscious of his appearance. If your character's desk is covered with bits of paper, he is obviously not very organised and we will not be surprised if, at some point in the story, he cannot find an important piece of paper upon which, perhaps, someone's life depends.

Traits

One of the differences between the novel and the short story is that the former needs fully-rounded main characters, revealing their complexities – their good qualities and their failings – whereas in the latter, there is only room to concentrate on one trait, showing it in action. A film director recently said that he could demolish a carefully built-up picture of a hardened killer by shooting a scene wherein the man reaches out to stroke a stray cat. This demonstrates how small 'brush-strokes' help define the different layers that go to make up a flesh-and-blood character and make the reader believe in his actions. In this case, it could be that his fondness for cats leads to his ultimate capture or death – because he hesitates too long between saving himself and saving the cat.

Generally speaking, aren't the characters we remember best those that were drawn larger than life? Think of Scarlett O'Hara, Bathsheba Everdene and Becky Sharp, for example.

Talking about creating characters in fiction, Somerset Maugham in *The Summing Up* tells of how he observed men, not for their own sake, but for the sake of his work. He was more concerned with the obscure than with the famous because the former were more often themselves (not putting on a public performance). He wrote: 'The ordinary is the writer's richer field. Its unexpectedness, its singularity, its infinite variety afford unending material. . . . the little man . . . is a bundle of contradictory elements. He is inexhaustible.'

Maugham often took persons whom he knew or had met and used them as the foundation for characters of his invention. Indeed, how can any writer help but do the same? Turgenev once stated that he could not create a character unless, as a starting point, he could fix his imagination on a living person, rather like a tiny piece of grit inside an oyster shell slowly being added to until it turns into a pearl.

I would suggest that each of our characters contains at least a part of ourselves. (Gustave Flaubert believed that, in creating Emma Bovary, his most famous character, he was embodying himself. 'Madame Bovary, c'est moi!' was his frequent cry.) Add to this a small part of someone we have known and blend with a large measure of imagination till we produce one who, though he or she exists solely within the pages of our story, is known to us as well as, if not better than, ourselves.

ROMAN A CLEF

Although most writers agree one should not, as a general rule in a work of fiction, take a character entirely from life, there is one notable exception: the *roman à clef* (literally meaning 'novel with a key'). In this type of novel, the real-life persons, and the events in which they were involved, are barely disguised as fiction. Dickens, for instance, based one of his best-known characters, Mr Micawber, on his father. Somerset Maugham portrayed a fellow author, Hugh Walpole, in *Cakes and Ale* while Edmund Spenser's *The Faerie Queene* was probably the first *roman à clef* ever published.

Somerset Maugham defended himself against criticisms that he drew on living people for his characters by pointing out that, 'From the beginning of literature authors have had originals for their creations.' However, it is not a practice to be advised, if only to guard against possible legal actions for libel, quite apart from accusations of lack of imagination.

Remember that details of dress, behaviour and mannerisms are only there to point up the basic nature of the people in your story. What has moulded them, made them into the sort of people they are, is what happened to them in childhood and the influence of parents, siblings, other relatives, teachers and friends. It is events and relationships *in the past*, before the story has begun, that have shaped them and dictate how they will behave under certain circumstances.

Because of the importance of creating in-depth main characters, especially in a novel, one way of getting to know them thoroughly is to keep a diary as if written by them. Let them write down their intimate thoughts and feelings, knowing no one else will ever read them. I guarantee you will learn a lot more about them, that way. Flaubert carried this a step further. Some of his characters made him so angry that he wrote whole scenes that were not meant to be included in his book but were just to relieve his feelings! But, as Virginia Woolf remarked, 'Novelists differ from the rest of the world because they do not cease to be interested in character when they have learnt enough about it for practical purposes.'

This need for believable, flesh-and-blood characters is stressed again and again by editors, and Pirandello said: 'When the characters are really alive before their author, the latter does nothing but follow them into their action, in their words, in the situations which they suggest to him.'

The Senior Editor of a well-known publisher of romantic novels has stated that characterisation is probably the most important element, and the toughest to do well, and that lack of credibility is a major reason for rejection. The successful story is one in which the protagonist *reacts characteristically* to the situations in which you, the writer, have placed him/her. It is their response to those circumstances that reveals them to the reader. As Chekhov said: 'A character's state of mind should be clear from his actions.'

Paul Gallico, describing how he set out to write a story that would sell, said that he invented likeable characters whom, in order for the reader to care about, he had to care deeply about, himself. Therefore, they had to have: 'echoing chords of his own hopes, fears, likes, dislikes, longings and appetites.'

MINOR CHARACTERS

So far, we have been discussing how to create major characters in a story but there will also be minor ones to consider. These neither need be, nor should be, drawn in the same detail. They are there to interact with your main characters, to be foils for them, to help you provide necessary information without recourse to such unsubtle means as having your heroine glance in a mirror and remark upon how wan she looks or how thick and lustrous her hair is. Here, the judicious use of a few 'brush-strokes' will bring them sufficiently to life.

Beware of introducing a minor character unless s/he has a role which is integral to the plot. Always ask yourself if you could possibly do without them and, if the answer is 'yes' – do just that!

DIALOGUE

Dialogue is probably the most important feature of good characterisation, as attested to by many well-known writers. In a television interview, the American playwright, Arthur Miller, told how, unless he can hear his characters speak, he can't create them. He went on to say that, in his early days as a writer, he always spoke their words out loud, often straining his voice in the process, but that, now, he is able to hear them in his head.

In the same interview, Arthur Miller commented that, unless he can identify with a character, he is unable to bring him to life. This is another way of saying that the writer must *become* that person: must get into his skin, know what he is thinking, feeling, contemplating doing. I wonder if the reason why so many beginner-writers say they find dialogue the hardest part of their work is that they have not been able to do this.

13

Dialogue, in fiction, has three basic functions to perform:

- To characterise
- To move the plot forward
- To impart necessary information.

When writing, use this check-list to ensure you have not allowed yourself to include waffle and irrelevant social chit-chat. If you find that you have, be ruthless and cut it out. For instance, suppose you have included a scene in a story in which your Main Character comes out of the house, walks down her garden path, spies her neighbour, Sally Johnson, trimming her roses and starts a conversation something like this:

> 'Morning, Sally. Thank goodness it's stopped raining. Quite a storm, though, wasn't it? I thought it was going to go on all day and I wouldn't be able to get out. I can't stand being in the house for hours at a time. Must have my constitutional. Not that I can go far, these days,' she added with a rueful laugh.
>
> Sally looked up and gave a vague nod. 'Yes. And just look at the damage it's done to my poor roses.'
>
> Jennifer Brown gave them a cursory glance. 'Well, must toddle. Get down to the shops in case it starts again.'

Unless it is vital that the reader knows it has been raining hard, that we need to be introduced to the next-door neighbour and that Jennifer is off to the shops, this part of the story could be cut. It is, however, typical of the kind of passage often found in beginners' stories. Even if you particularly wanted to establish that the neighbour was in the garden as Jennifer went out, this could be done without giving her a speaking part. For example:

> I'll bet that Sally is in the garden again, now the rain's stopped, snip, snip, snipping at those damned roses. I'll never manage to slip past without her seeing me. Jennifer gave her head an irritable shake as she thrust her arms into the sleeves of her coat

Another thing we are often told, when we start to write, is that dialogue helps break up the narrative and improves the look of the page, important because many readers are put off by huge chunks of narrative. True enough – but the dialogue must be there for a purpose – and part of the writer's skill lies in devising a scene that will have one.

Let's suppose the first version is necessary for your story, and examine it to see if it fulfils the three functions of dialogue:

Characterise In it, we do learn something about both people. Jennifer Brown is clearly an active person, but getting on in years. She's also cheerful because she's able to laugh wryly at her ageing limbs. Sally is a keen gardener and obviously more interested in her roses than her neighbour.

Move the story forward Here it falls down. Jennifer Brown could easily have glanced through her kitchen window, spied her neighbour in the garden, realised it had stopped raining and decided to go for a walk where, presumably, she will meet someone or where something will happen to her. It is doubtful that Sally has an important role to play in the story.

Provide necessary information This function is just possibly fulfilled, provided we need to know that Sally is in the garden with her roses, that Jennifer is going shopping and that it has been raining heavily. Here again, however, more than likely it could all have been imparted through Jennifer's thoughts while in her kitchen, thus dispensing with her interaction with the second character altogether. For example:

> Jennifer opened her front door and peered out with a myopic stare. The rain must have stopped completely, she thought, because surely that was Sally next door, snipping away at the roses that drooped over the fence between the gardens?

Going back to characterisation, an interesting (and useful) exercise is to write the same scenario but involving different characters, because the language they use will depend upon their age, sex, background and so on. Or, imagine a retired English teacher, refusing an invitation to a celebration of some kind. Then think of how a 17-year-old boy, a middle-aged housewife and a 'yuppy' might all respond. Without describing them, we ought to be able to pick up sufficient clues from what they say, from the actual words they use, their juxtaposition, the sentence structure, to learn something about them.

If the teacher said: 'Kind it is of you to ask,' you could fairly deduce he was Welsh. If a character replied: 'Sorry, mate. Got something else on, tonight.' I think you could rightly suppose it was a young man speaking in the vernacular of today.

Dialogue increases pace

When writing fiction, it is well to remember that most of us tend to live in the fast-lane in today's world. We're used to getting our news instantly and visually through television: to 'seeing' a good deal of our fiction on the 'box'. Therefore, on the whole, modern novels have far more dialogue than they used to *because it increases the pace:* it helps create immediacy, the illusion that *we are there*. We prefer to be fed necessary information in short snatches of dialogue. To those who would argue that they still enjoy reading the classics, often with long descriptive passages, such as novels by Thomas Hardy, Charles Dickens, Leo Tolstoy or Charlotte Bronte, and ask why they shouldn't, themselves, write in the same style, I would unhesitatingly state that those same authors, being professionals, if alive today, would be writing in the style of their contemporaries and not in that of yesteryear.

Alternatives to 'said'

The use of alternative speech tags to 'said' (he warned; she chanted; he burst out; and so on), if used judiciously, can provide extra information about the particular character's reactions to the situation. It would not be wise to overload a piece of writing with these but they can be useful to point up the way in which the words are uttered, the way the character is feeling; it is really a matter of choice. Some teachers of creative writing say they should never be used – but I don't agree. I compiled a list of more than one hundred of them which you might find of interest. I hadn't realised just how many there were until I began noting them down! (See page 118.)

Bits of action, tacked on to speech, also impart more information, such as:

As he finished speaking, heavy lids descended, veiling piercing black orbs.

He emphasised his words with an extravagant flourish of his hand.

Her eyes flashed fire as she spoke.

Thus, using dialogue enables you to avoid long-winded sections of narrative, while getting across the same information. It is so vital a tool that, in the notebook I keep when I'm working on a particular piece of fiction, I have a note at the front which asks in big letters: CAN IT BE TOLD IN DIALOGUE? to remind myself of its importance.

Write by ear, not by eye

Another essential for writing effective dialogue (and something many of us find it difficult to do) is to set aside the rules of grammar that were instilled in us at school. We must write dialogue 'as it is spoke'. Again, we come back to characterisation because, if we want readers to believe in the character, we should be putting the right words into his or her mouth. If s/he says: 'I cannot'; 'I will not'; or 'I am unable to', then that should be because s/he is a pedantic, extremely formal person. Mostly, however, we use contractions in our speech: 'I can't'; 'I won't'; 'I'm not able to'. If we read all our dialogue aloud, as Arthur Miller suggests we should, we will quickly hear if it sounds wrong and can then correct it.

Similarly, if we are creating a rather uneducated character, we can drop in occasional ungrammatical phrases such as: 'I don't know who done it. It weren't me.' And, while we all know we should never use clichés or hackneyed phrases in narrative, if the character we are building is the sort who would use them, then we can, and should, put them into his mouth. The same applies to using expletives. If you are creating someone who would use swear words, then put one or two into his mouth. Today, it is no longer necessary to substitute a row of dots. If you dislike writing such language, then it is best to avoid introducing such a character. Indeed, you could hardly hope to bring him to life because you could not identify with him.

Another useful trick, especially when writing for radio, is to give your main character a particular turn of phrase, or a physical trait that can be referred to, occasionally – for instance, the tapping of a walking-stick or clicking of knitting needles – that will readily identify him/her to the listener.

The rhythm of words is important, too, in narrative as well as dialogue and I believe you should 'hear' all your writing in your head, even if you don't say it aloud, to ensure it flows smoothly. With dialogue, though, this is particularly important and, often, only needs a word cutting or adding or its position changing to make it sound better.

Thoughts

These are used in the same way as dialogue, that is, to fulfill the same functions and also break up chunks of narrative. Nowadays, they are usually not put in quotes, though that is up to you. In any case, a publisher will have house rules that may dictate how they appear in the printed work.

Speech tags

Often these can be omitted, though only if it is obvious who is speaking. For example:

'I just don't believe it.' Mary's eyes widened in horror.

'Well, it's true. Jimmy told me so himself.' Dinah tried, and failed, to keep her voice steady.

'In that case . . . ' Mary stood up and purposefully fastened her coat. 'I'll be on the very next train to Melchester. And then we'll see.'

This little scene avoided the 'she saids' by using, instead, action to delineate who was speaking and, at the same time, provided more information about what was happening.

Dialect

Use dialect sparingly and only to add a touch of local colour because most of us, today, become irritated by too much of it. It is far better to use words peculiar to a certain region rather than difficult-to-read-and-say dialect. In Yorkshire, for instance, people use the word 'while' instead of 'until' – I won't be there while morning. 'Hinny' is a Geordie expression for a young girl while, in Devon, they frequently say 'maid'. West Indians often add 'man' to their speech: what you doing there, man?

Setting out dialogue

The following is an example of how to set out dialogue in your typescript, how to show speech within a speech, how to show thoughts and how to use action to add extra information and avoid over-use of speech tags:

'There's nothing more to be said.' May folded her gloved hands neatly on her lap.

'But there is. You don't understand. It isn't like it sounds. Please, for God's sake, let me explain.'

'No. It's finished. Over. Leave it like that.' She rose and, with exaggerated care, brushed a speck of fluff off her expensively-tailored black skirt. 'When Delia rang and said, "You'll not thank me for telling you this, May dear, but I simply can't let Gerard go on deceiving you any longer," I knew it was true. I'd known all along, really.' I just hadn't wanted to, she thought, with silent, bitter honesty.

'You're always so damned clinical,' he burst out. 'It's like you take a scalpel, sterilise it, then cut. Finito!'

May permitted a tiny sigh to escape her lips. Was that really how he saw her, she wondered? Was it how all the others had seen her? Well, it was too late to change, now. She must just accept herself for what she was. And, if others couldn't – well, that was *their* problem. She stood up. 'I'm sorry, Gerard, but that's how it is. If you'd only come to me, weeks ago, and said: "I don't know how to tell you this, May, but, if there's to be any future for us, I must," maybe things could have been different. As it is . . . ' She shrugged and, without giving him another glance, walked swiftly away, out of the room and out of his life. For ever.

VIEWPOINT

It is vitally important to understand what viewpoint means and how to handle it in your stories. In order to do this, it is necessary, first of all, to understand its significance. Once you have grasped that, you will know exactly what you are doing – and why. You will be able to make a rational decision before you start work on a piece of fiction – or reverse the decision, later, if it doesn't seem to be working out.

The reason why viewpoint is so important when writing fiction is that our aim is to produce the strongest possible effect we can with the materials we have. And our materials are words and the way we use them. Certainly, we want to write to the best of our ability so that those who read it will admire our skill, enjoy our tale. But, unless we have *moved* them, involved them in the lives of our characters, no matter how superb our style, our choice of language, our descriptive passages, we will have failed. Indeed, we're unlikely to have any readers.

Therefore, we need to use every technique at our disposal. We need to consciously ask ourselves – will it work better this way – or that? Will it be best told from this viewpoint or that? If, having weighed up the pros and cons of using first or third person you decide you would feel happier telling this particular short story (or particular scene in your novel) through the eyes of Main Character Joanna Benton, then, unless you have a very good reason for changing mid-way, you should *stick to her viewpoint throughout*. And the only possible reason for not doing so is that you have made a conscious decision because you feel it will improve your story. With amateurs, the changing of viewpoint from one character to another is often totally unconscious but it considerably weakens the story.

Why should a single viewpoint strengthen a story and a multiple viewpoint weaken it? The reason lies in never forgetting what is possibly the most important single element in any work of fiction – emotion – moving the reader to laughter, tears, dislike, fear and so on.

Let me illustrate this point. Someone tells you about the tragic case of a mother forced to watch, helplessly, while her only child drowns. Instantly, all your emotions are engaged; you empathise with her terrible situation. If *you* are a mother, you will experience some of her pain and anguish and tremble at the thought of its ever happening to you. Now, suppose the narrator of that tale of sorrow breaks off and starts to relate how she or someone else standing on the river bank felt. Your mind and your emotions have to make a sudden switch and the tension is reduced. How a less-involved onlooker felt doesn't affect you nearly so much.

In fiction, your aim is to increase the tension at the high points of the story, even to the point at which the reader cannot bear it any longer and you have to let him or her off the hook for a while. But do it too quickly, and without good reason, and the reader will be irritated. 'I was just getting involved with how *she* was feeling and now I've got to start all over again trying to experience how *he* feels.' Surely, an understandable reaction – and one to be avoided.

Basically, there are three viewpoints to choose from: first person, third person and omniscient (or god's eye, meaning 'having infinite knowledge') and not to be confused with that error ever to be avoided known as 'author intrusion' – for example, sentences like: The mores of those times were quite different to those of today.

Whichever viewpoint you opt for in order to tell your story, it will have advantages and disadvantages. So, let's study them all, in turn.

First person

An example of this would be: I looked at Jim and, despite the pain clawing at my heart, I knew I could never leave him.

It helps create *immediacy*. You, the narrator, are *there*: you are relating events as they happened to you. The reader is then carried along with it, believing everything you say.

First person is particularly effective in building up suspense, which is why authors like Mary Stewart and Phyllis Whitney use this form in their immensely successful romantic suspense novels. It removes the barrier between author and reader: it is *I* telling *you* about the frightening, exciting or wonderful things that happened to me. And you believe them.

Have you ever been caught out by one of those jokes that are successful only if told by someone with a dead-pan face? One, by someone recently returned from a visit to the States, had such a 'ring of truth' that it took me in completely. It depended for its effectiveness on my believing in the circumstances of his standing in a queue at a supermarket check-out and being 'conned' into paying for someone else's groceries.

As it was told as if it had actually happened to him, I totally suspended any disbelief. In a word – immediacy – because it was related in the first person.

A second advantage is that it is almost impossible to slip, unknowingly, from first to third person. In fact, if you find sticking to a single viewpoint a problem, initially, a neat trick is to write your story in the first, then change it to the third when you've finished. A good exercise, too.

Its main disadvantage is that it precludes you from seeing or knowing what any of the other characters could see or know, from going into their thoughts or knowing what is happening elsewhere. However, there are ways to get round this because you can *guess* what someone else is thinking by their facial expressions or body-language. You can *imagine* what is happening out of sight behind the rocks. Mary Stewart conveys this kind of information superbly well.

Here are some examples of my own of how you can get over this problem:

> I stared up into Martin's face, devoid of all expression, except for a momentary glint of . . . of what, I asked myself? Fear? Anger? Wariness? I let my gaze drop to his hands and saw they were clenched and sweating. And then I knew. Martin was afraid. Very afraid.

> The sound, slight at first, grew as it echoed across the bare, bleak hillside. I turned slowly in the direction it came from and, with a sense of foreboding, my eyes focused on the dark rock face beyond. And I knew, for certain, that Luke Chisholm was there. Waiting.

To get across the first person narrator's own state of mind, apart from constantly saying 'I thought' or 'I felt', there are various devices, though they should be used subtly and with discretion:

> I gazed around the room, almost with a stranger's eyes, noting the gaudy splashes of colour made by the cushions on the low beige-leather couch, cushions against which, only moments before, *he* had been resting

> I stared at my tear-smudged face in the mirror and wondered if I could ever smile again.

Once you have started a novel in the first person, you cannot change part-way through. I say 'cannot' because only an accomplished writer is likely to be able to bring off such a change. The only novel I can think of in which the method was employed was *Bowhani Junction* by John Masters, where he told the story in separate sections, one narrated by the 'I' and the others from the viewpoint of different characters.

Third person

An example of this viewpoint would be:

Ellie looked at Jim and, despite the pain clawing at her heart, she knew she could never leave him.

Writing in the third person, that is from the angle character's viewpoint – by far the most common one used in fiction – still means the reader can only know what that character knows or is thinking. (The 'angle character' is the person through whose eyes the incidents of the story are seen and whose story is unfolding.)

Joanna Benton, sitting in a chair in her kitchen, cannot know what her husband is thinking, seated beside her or, for certain, what her daughter is doing up in her bedroom even if she can hear the ghetto-blaster from downstairs. She might be doing her homework or sewing – or reading – at the same time and her mother couldn't know that. The main advantage of using the third person is that, within the constraints already outlined, you can write from the angle of several characters (that is, multiple viewpoint). Most novels make use of this facility to tell the story and this is perfectly permissible; indeed, it is often desirable.

Again, however, apply caution and make a rational decision (because you believe it will *strengthen* your story, as previously explained), before changing viewpoint.

Omniscient

In this final example, it is the god on high who is observing and telling the reader what Ellie's reactions are to the situation she finds herself in:

Who could have known, as Ellie stared at the man before her, that pain was clawing at her heart? That she was telling herself she could never leave him?

This viewpoint is not often used in the short story because it is impersonal and objective and, therefore, does not engage the emotions as do the other two viewpoints. Invariably, though, it will be used at certain points in a novel, usually where exposition – an explanation of whatever in

24

the past led your characters to what is happening now – is needed.

Clearly, from which character's viewpoint the story will be told is a very important decision which has to be taken before starting to write a piece of fiction.

EMOTION

'Biting my truant pen, beating myself for spite,
"Fool," said my Muse to me, "look in thy heart and write."'

Sir Philip Sidney

Paul Gallico said: 'To sell, it is only necessary to capture the human imagination and *touch the human heart*' (my italics) – and he was an author who knew how to do just that.

The word 'emotion' comes from the same root as motivation – from *movere*, to move – and what we writers of fiction must do is to move our readers so that they weep, shudder with horror or laugh out loud with our characters according to the situations in which we put them. The books we most remember tend to be those that moved us deeply and where we identified with what the characters were feeling.

The editorial director of a large publishing house, addressing a group of writers, suggested that, rather than keeping in mind the maxim 'Write about what you know', a better one might be to 'Write about what you *feel*'. We should then be better able to transfer our own emotions to our characters.

A simple technique to help convey feeling in a particular scene is to write down the key word for it. For example, fear or dread, regret, sorrow, humour, then list all the words you can think of that describe or add to that emotion (you might also look in a thesaurus). Using some of these words in the text will help you to create the right atmosphere.

Another way is to go into your character's thoughts so that we know, subjectively, how he/she is feeling.

Emotive themes

There are certain themes which, if introduced into a novel or a short story, cannot fail to arouse an emotional response in the reader. Among these are the following:

* Rejection
* Loneliness
* Pain of being misunderstood
* Death of a loved one – human or animal
* Enforced separation from a loved one, an animal or place
* A feeling of always being on the outside, looking in.

Did you, like me, cry buckets over books/films like Marjorie Rawlings' *The Yearling*? I've seen grown men become moist-eyed watching *Lassie Come Home* and *E.T.* When my daughter was very young, I remember her coming home from school and sobbing so inconsolably that I thought something terrible must have happened. Finally, I managed to discover that her teacher had been reading the story of the faithful hound, Bedgellert, whose master slew him, not realising until too late that the dog had saved his child's life from the wolf (or snake – depending on which version you've read).

The reason we can be so affected by these themes is that most of us, at some time in our lives, have known the devastation of feeling unwanted, of not being understood, of being an outsider. At a deep level, we live through that experience, again, identifying with the fictional character.

Tolstoy also had one or two things to say about emotion in writing. One should ' . . . evoke in oneself a sensation which one has experienced before, and having evoked it in oneself, to communicate this sensation in such a way that others may experience the same sensation . . . ' And 'Real art depends first on feeling.'

In any dramatic scene, emotion should be present. Someone must want something, must be motivated to take some action, whether through fear, hatred, jealousy, love or whatever. I have never suffered a serious burn but my imagination can graphically horrify me with pictures of what it must be like. Therefore, when reading a novel in which the main character – a young woman – is threatened with branding by her father (who, having escaped from prison, was bent on revenge for having been sent there), I experienced a *frisson* of horror at such a foul deed, an emotion further heightened because it was the girl's father bent on doing this to her. For a few moments, all disbelief was suspended as I 'lived through' that scene. The writer had done her job well. She had drawn me into it: I was *there*!

If you want to write a bestseller, you would be wise to ensure that at least one of those powerfully emotive elements I've mentioned are included. Consider the themes of some novels that have made fortunes for their authors, often being turned into films for screen or television. A high proportion are about a poor boy or girl making good, rising from an under-privileged background and overcoming great odds to succeed in the world of Big Business. I suppose such novels are immensely popular because, although most of us will never really be wealthy, we like to read stories about someone who has 'made it'. Deep down, we can allow ourselves to think: Who knows, maybe, one day, it could happen to me.

To capture that essential ingredient – emotion – and include it in our fiction realistically, we need to reach down into the well of our own memories of grief, of joy, of unrequited love – and dredge them up into our consciousness. That may be a painful process. Can you, if you push aside the healing veil of time, live again that knife-thrust of rejection, of betrayal? Or the intensity of first falling in love? If you can, and you can transmit those feelings on to paper, you stand a much greater chance of success. Virginia Woolf said that strong emotion must leave its trace and that 'The pen gets on the scent'.

Sentimentality

Don't confuse emotion with sentimentality; the latter is superficial – it has no genuine depth. I have heard it described as being 'emotion without commitment or responsibility', which about sums it up. Think of the politician who, smiling indulgently, pats a baby's head during an

27

election campaign. However much we may applaud his politics, we cringe at the obvious falseness of the display of affection. We know that, if the baby were to be suddenly sick, he would hastily thrust it from him. Or the woman who fusses over the enchanting puppy but who would run a mile rather than clean up after it before it was house-trained. Both are examples of mawkish sentimentality.

To be truly moved, either in real life or through a work of fiction, we have to be able to experience vicariously the event or happening being depicted. And, in order for the writer to bring that about, he will have to show (not tell) within a scene the effect of that incident upon his character. He must create a dramatic scene, a unit of action, that affects his character strongly. If he writes of babies or puppies, young love, death, war or peace en masse, he is in danger of sentimentalising. If he writes of one particular baby, puppy, young man in love; one woman coping with bereavement, the effects of war or a peace that comes too late to prevent a loved one from dying, he is more likely to invoke true emotion.

Lastly, remember the power of understatement. By having *suggested* something to the reader, often one can then leave the rest to his imagination. But, whatever you write about, never forget that the reader loves to cry – or to shudder or laugh.

CONFLICT

Conflict is inherent in every story; indeed, without it, there *is* no story. But what does the word mean? My dictionary defines it as 'a coming into collision'.

We've already considered the need to introduce emotion into our fiction and some of the most emotive themes. In every one of these, conflict is bound to be present. It is there whenever someone desperately wants something and there are obstacles in the way: for instance, wanting to belong to a person, or group, and being rejected; wanting to explain certain circumstances and not being believed; trying, and failing, to save someone or something he/she deeply loves;

and so on. If two characters are bound together in some way, but with two opposing goals, that, too, is bound to result in conflict.

For anyone reading this who may dislike conflict in real life and will go to any lengths to avoid it, let me stress that, in fiction, it does not have to equate with physical violence. It can be, and often is, merely an intense longing for something abstract, such as regaining one's good name or wanting to be thought well of. But circumstances, another person or a 'fatal flaw' in one's own nature (perhaps foolishness, pride or selfishness), are obstacles preventing its attainment.

Types of conflict

There are three types of conflict – in life as well as in fiction:

* Man against man (external)
* Man against nature (external)
* Man against himself (internal).

You will strengthen your story considerably if you can bring both internal and external conflict into the same scene.
The man faced with the swollen river which he must cross if he is to save his wife's life, but who is also terrified of water because he nearly drowned as a child, faces both internal and external conflict (man against himself – fear of drowning; man against nature – the swollen river). Thus the conflict is doubled and the tension heightened.

The desired goal must be of the utmost importance to your character *at that moment in time*, and all his energies, mental and physical, must be directed into trying to achieve that end.

Conflict between relatives, lovers, close friends, or between people of different cultures or backgrounds also increases tension. Alfred Uhry used the latter two in his Pulitzer Prize-winning play (later turned into a very successful film), *Driving Miss Daisy*. It is, basically, a gentle story about friendship and trust developing over many years between two diametrically-opposed people. One, an elderly, white, wealthy Jewess; the other, an elderly, poor, Christian Negro who becomes her chauffeur and general handyman.

If that play had been about an elderly, white, Christian woman and an elderly, white, Christian manservant, the resulting conflict would not have been anything like so strong without any overt violence taking place.

The fuel of fiction

I once heard conflict described as the fuel which drives the engine of the story till it reaches its conclusion: a good analogy, I think.

Never lose sight of the fact that conflict must be rooted firmly in motivation. Whatever your character wants and whatever obstacles you, the writer, have placed in his path, the conflict will be weakened, even lost, unless his desire is so strong that it *forces him to act* to overcome those obstacles.

SHOW, DON'T TELL
(INDIRECT EXPOSITION)

This maxim is one most writers will have often heard and, next to 'write about what you know', it is probably the most useful one to remember and put into practice. Write in scenes that let the reader *see* what is happening whenever you are describing an important piece of action.

To do this, you will always need to introduce dialogue (or interior monologue). Wherever possible, you should employ the five senses of touch, taste, smell, hearing and seeing to build a vivid picture in the reader's mind. Straight 'telling' is perhaps the most frequent trap the beginner fiction-writer falls into. Often, s/he doesn't realise why the story hasn't been successful and can't see why until someone explains. Here are some brief examples.

Gemma was suddenly filled with fear. Her feet refused to move, as if they were literally rooted to the spot. She wanted to run but daren't, certain that *he* was there, lurking in the shadows, waiting to reach out and grab her, if she did.

This 'tells' us that Gemma is desperately afraid, that she thinks someone she knows is hiding in the dark ready to waylay her, but it certainly doesn't 'show' us her fear or tell us very much about where she is, what is happening or why. It would be far more effective if it were expanded into a scene on the following lines:

> Gemma jerked to a halt and froze. 'Who's there?' she croaked, her mouth suddenly dry. No one answered – but her ears, strained to catch the tiniest sound, heard a faint rustle from the furthest corner of the room, shrouded in gloom. The corner nearest the door. It's him! He's here, I know he is, she thought, her heart pounding inside her ribcage, like a drum beating the retreat. Only there was no retreat for her. At least, not unless she took a risk and made a run for it. But that's what he's waiting for, she warned herself, feeling the sweat break out across her brow. Then he'll reach out and grab me. And a sob burst from her lips.

Without actually saying Gemma is afraid, we've *shown* it by her dry mouth, her pricked ears, her pounding heart and her sweating brow. Because, at some time in our own lives, we have experienced those same sensations, we *know* exactly how she is feeling. Our imaginations will supply all the rest. 'Showing' is an effective way of describing a character's feelings, of getting emotion into a scene.

You will only need to develop important scenes in this way. If, as we suspect but aren't yet sure, Gemma is worrying unnecessarily (although, obviously, she has good reason to fear him, whoever he is) and you then force her to run the gauntlet, discover no human is lurking in the shadows but that it was probably only a mouse she'd heard, you will have allowed the tension to drop a little. You can then revert to straight narrative, thus:

> Gemma's heartbeat slowly returned to normal and a rueful smile touched her lips as she hastened homewards to the

safety of her cottage. Chagrined, she told herself that, once again, she'd let her stupid imagination get the better of her. All the same, she thought, she'd still lock and bolt the doors and windows, that night, just to be sure.

Here is another example – of how *not* to do it:

James Robinson suddenly felt 30 years younger as he found himself kicking the ball to the encouraging cries of the boys in the street. This was because, for the first time since he'd retired, he'd actually tried to talk to them instead of ticking them off as he usually did.

Instead, it would be better to write it something like this:

'Come on, grandad,' the boy taunted. 'Let's see yous score a goal like you keep telling us you used te.'

James Robinson straightened his shoulders and, in one quick movement, tossed aside the stick he'd carried since his retirement. As he did so, a grin spread across his lined face because, along with the stick, he felt he was tossing away the past 30 years. 'O.K. young fella-me-lad,' he muttered beneath his breath, 'You're on.' And, as his lowered head came into contact with the wonderful round leather shape of the ball, he let out a whoop of sheer joy.

There are a few signs to watch out for in your MS which can warn you you may be about to commit the sin of 'telling'. Mostly, these are if you find yourself writing words and phrases like: because; just then; and so; the reason was. If you do, pull yourself up sharply and take a good look at what you're doing. It may be perfectly legitimate to use one of these expressions at that point in your story – but stopping to examine it could just make you realise the danger.

For example:

As Mary set off down the road, she felt a pang of guilt. The reason was because she'd left her sister behind, confined in her wheelchair, the way she was every day, now.

Or:

Just then, a man in a dark brown suit ran out of the shop.

Or, another example:

And so John decided to go straight home instead of stopping off to see Lorna.

Try to write a scene, using one of these examples. You
might even find it sparks off a story in your mind but, at
least, it will serve as a reminder, next time you're about to fall
into the trap of 'telling' instead of 'showing'. Finally, why not
put a notice above your desk: CAN I MAKE A SCENE OF
IT?

BUILDING TENSION

Tension is closely linked with suspense but, whereas suspense is a state of uncertainty, of apprehensive expectation,
tension is the act of stretching or the state of being
stretched. So, in order to build tension in a story, we have to
keep the reader in suspense about what will happen next for
as long as is possible without him or her becoming impatient
or irritated. Then it will be necessary to reduce the tension a
little, rather like playing a fish on a line when, for a few
moments, you let it think it's getting away before slowly
reeling it in again.
  Tension, in fiction, is created when powerful forces op-
pose each other until one side or the other has to give way,
either totally or partially. Always, there will be something at
stake. Your Main Character will gain or lose something of
importance as a result of what is happening or is about to
happen.
  Think of a piece of elastic; there is a point beyond which it
cannot be stretched further or it will break and the tension
will be lost forever. Similarly, there comes a point in a story
where you must relax the tension a little before you increase

33

it again. But it will have served its purpose in the suspenseful continuum of the story. The reader will know that there is more to come: that the protagonist's dilemma is anything but over. To give an example, let's go back to the previous section, *Show, Don't Tell*, and take another look at the scene in which Gemma is terrified someone is waiting to grab her.

She hears a sound coming from the dark corner of the room and thinks: It's him! He's here . . . Immediately, the reader also experiences her fear, not knowing whether or not *he* (whoever he is) is really there. When Gemma manages to overcome it and discovers it was her imagination playing tricks, the tension is slackened. But a doubt has been planted in the reader's mind. Who is this mysterious man she is afraid of? Is he going to find her, later in the story? Instinctively, because fiction follows a definite pattern, we know that he is, otherwise he would not have been introduced. However, a beginner might possibly have included that scene in a mistaken attempt to create suspense without any intention of using it again. In that case, it would have stood in isolation and the reader, discovering this later on, would have felt cheated and frustrated.

We have been given a broad hint, in this scene, that someone is out to get Gemma, for whatever reason. We have seen her relief at finding she was alone and we have also learned she is going to make sure her cottage is locked and bolted, that night, so we *know* her fear has not gone away completely. It is going to resurface before long and we suspect *he* is going to break into the cottage, maybe that very night.

The tension has been relaxed – but only slightly. The suspense of 'what happens next?' (which is what storytelling is all about) remains.

Varying tension

There are various ways of building and relaxing tension, at the same time maintaining the suspense. In a novel (where change of viewpoint is permissible), one way is to let the reader know something your character does not. We all remember how, in a pantomime at Christmas or at a Punch and Judy show on the beach, the young audience sees the villain creeping up behind the unaware hero or Mr Punch, and starts yelling to warn him. You can use this same ploy in a story.

For instance, in a murder mystery or a psychological thriller, we can know that the man following the woman in the park, after dusk, is stalking his potential victim. We can know he has a knife in his pocket. We can see her quicken her pace as she realises someone appears to be following her. We can see him do the same. Then she breaks into a run, her breath coming faster and faster as she tries to get away. Then, maybe she stumbles and almost falls, allowing the man to catch up with her. She turns, her face glistening with fear – then she laughs in nervous relief as she recognises him as someone she knows well. 'Oh, it's you. You scared me half to death.' Only, we know something she doesn't. We know he has a knife hidden away and we're pretty sure he's been following her for some awful purpose she isn't aware of.

In this way, the piece of elastic is stretched further and further up to the point that the potential victim recognises her pursuer, then it is allowed to slacken – but only slightly. The reader is still uneasy, still wondering what's going to happen next. And when s/he finds out, when that question is answered, the writer must instantly pose another – at least as fingernail-biting as the last.

It is possible to reduce tension by introducing a touch of humour that makes your character smile or laugh and subtly alters the situation that is developing. Or by breaking off to describe the fairly unexceptional surroundings in order to fool both your character and your reader.

Evelyn Anthony, Phyllis Whitney, Mary Stewart all brilliantly employ tension and suspense and are well worth studying. In Evelyn Anthony's *The Legend*, one of the characters, the Countess, is at the airport, returning to England with a vital piece of information. She has discovered that one of the British Secret Service's most respected members is a traitor. A man, carrying a raincoat over his arm, comes to sit beside her in the airport lounge. Immediately, we wonder: is he significant or is he just a bit

35

of background colour? We suspect the former. If something is specifically brought to our attention, it's for a reason – and the piece of elastic starts to tauten. Then the man is mentioned again, and the tension grows. When his presence is referred to yet again, we *know* something is going to happen involving him and the Countess but we aren't sure what. Is he going to succeed in silencing her before she can divulge her lethal information in England? Cleverly, Ms Anthony relaxes the elastic just a fraction, letting the Countess fall asleep and miss her plane, before she gives it a final tug. She extracts every last bit of suspense out of that particular scene before she lets us off the hook. That is the way to keep the reader's full attention. Just when s/he thinks s/he can't bear any more, give one last jerk.

The 'time bomb' technique

Another favoured method, this is equally effective in either the short story or the novel: the Main Character has to solve his problem or achieve his goal *within a specified time* – or else! If the hero doesn't manage to cross the swollen river before dark, it will be too late to save his wife who is dying. If the heroine can't find the piece of paper that will prove her father's innocence, he will be hanged. If the young hero can't free himself from the fallen rock inside the cave before the incoming tide sweeps in, he will drown. And, if he drowns, his sister will be forced into an arranged marriage with a man she loathes. In other words, you keep a sword of Damocles hanging over your character's head until you are ready to remove it – or let it fall.

Life crisis

Similarly, you can deliberately introduce something of great import to your main character, something that could well affect the rest of his life. For instance, in an historical romance one of my students was writing, the heroine's father is in jail awaiting trial and, if found guilty, could be sentenced to transportation. If that were to happen, how would Sophie, a well-bred young lady, manage without a man to take care of her? Previously, she's never had to consider her financial position: now, all that has changed. Because, by this time, the hero has entered the story, we are aware that she might have to consider marriage as a way out of her difficulties. Or will she, instead, find this new situation a challenge and decide to fly in the face of society's mores at that time and opt for independence? Either way, her father's impending trial has important implications for her and increases the suspense.

Foreshadowing conflict

An ominous dark cloud looming on the horizon, for instance, can suggest coming conflict and introduce tension. Careful choice of words also helps. 'A scowl etched itself across his brow like a far-off warning rumble of thunder', should hint at trouble not very far ahead for someone.

The 'magic three' or repetition

Think of all the children's games and fairy-tales which depend on repeating something three times in ever-increasing intensity with the avowed intent of inducing fear. These range from the simple 'Round and round the garden, like a teddy-bear. One step, two steps . . . tickle you under there!' played with a very small child, to *Goldilocks and the Three Bears*, the *Three Billy Goats Gruff*, *Little Red Riding Hood, Hansel and Gretel* to those spine-chilling tales by the Brothers Grimm. This same device was used by W.W. Jacobs in his classic horror story, *The Monkey's Paw*, and by Edgar Allan Poe, that other master of spine-tingling horror.

Cliff-hanger

One must never forget the 'cliff-hanger' which was used to such effect in those serials some of us may remember seeing at Saturday afternoon cinema, when we were children. Remember *Tonto and The Lone Ranger* and the exciting music that accompanied the serial, each episode of which left one of them in deadly danger? How could anyone bear

37

to miss going the following week to see how they extricated themselves? Although these were always melodramatic situations, the principle holds good for all story-telling. This same technique should be employed, whenever possible, at the end of every chapter and, in the case of a magazine serial, at the end of every instalment.

Will she, won't she?

Walter Allen, in *The English Novel*, refers to another form of suspense frequently employed in bestselling fiction known as 'the principle of procrastinated rape'. In it, he describes how Samuel Richardson, in his novel *Pamela*, has the protagonist, Mr B, in hot pursuit of Pamela's virginity. 'Will she lose it? Will she? Won't she? The suspense is everything; and the screw is turned to the uttermost,' he says.

Surprise only happens once

C.P. Snow, when reviewing one of John le Carré's novels, said about suspense that it '. . . will remain just as taut every time one reads it (the novel). Surprise, though, happens only once. After the first reading, it has gone forever.' How true that is. However, even though one knows perfectly well how a particular story will end, or even the result of a real-life battle or incident which has been dramatised, a good writer will so cleverly maintain the tension, build up the suspense that, right up to the end, part of us will still hope that, this time, it will be different: that, if we cry out to the character, warn him of what is about to happen, somehow it won't. If you can create a tension, a suspense so great that the reader can't bear to put your novel or story down but simply has to turn the page and read on, you have found the secret of successful fiction-writing and demonstrated craftsmanship at its best.

DESCRIPTION/BACKGROUND/ ATMOSPHERE

I've put these three together because they are so closely linked.

Long descriptive passages are a thing of the past: today's readers have neither the time nor the patience for them. Therefore, whenever you include them, you have to make them work hard for you. They should paint in the background of the story, elicit some emotional response in the reader and be an integral part of the story, not merely an embellishment. They should also be painted vividly and briefly.

A description of a threatening storm or a deserted landscape or a brilliant summer's day should convey something more to the reader than a mere picture of the setting. In the first two, the reader should experience an inner shiver of apprehension and a feeling that something is going to happen. In the latter, all is well for the character involved, at least for the moment. If a tiny cloud appears far off on the horizon, however, we know trouble of some kind is on its way before long.

CHOICE OF WORDS

Scenes of action generally need sharper, shorter words and strong verbs: he shot across the room; his feet drummed on the hard ground; she spat the words at him as she tore herself free. On the other hand, a sexual encounter between hero and heroine will be made more sensuous by the use of sibilants: silent, scintillate, smooth, silken, shimmer and so on. Similarly, an eerie place needs to be described in words we associate with feeling scared, such as: creek, shudder, groan, wail, murmur, shadows.

Sensory details, *plus* the character's emotional reaction, will help produce the desired response in the reader. For instance, descriptions of the weather at a particular moment in your story can echo your character's mood, which will be transmitted to the reader.

William Faulkner once said that: 'A writer needs three things – experience, observation and imagination.' To write memorable descriptions, ability to observe is an essential attribute for the writer. And, without a vividly-drawn background and creating the necessary atmosphere through the right choice of words, your characters will act out their story in a vacuum. (See also *Style*, later in this section.)

FLASHBACKS

It is almost impossible to avoid the use of flashback in fiction because what has happened to our characters in the past (as with ourselves) is influencing their actions at the point at which the story opens and as it continues to develop. The construction of some types of short story (the 'true-life' or 'confession' story, for example) are wholly dependent upon the flashback for their impact.

You may have read, or been told, that long flashbacks should never be used but I think that is too didactic, at least where the novel is concerned. 'If it works, it works' is a good maxim – but be sure that it does and that it isn't holding up the story.

The flashback is a device for interrupting the narrative in order to show or explain past events. A good writer can slip into one so unobtrusively that, a few sentences into it, the reader will forget that that particular piece of action took place months or years previously and will absorb it *as if it were happening now*. That is the trick: to make it seem like it is happening now.

One way to make it effective is only to introduce it *after* you have promised some future action and excitement. For example: Emma is about to leave the home where she's lived ever since the death of her mother. Her cousin, Thomas, to whom she has just become engaged, has mysteriously disappeared and she is determined to find him. She has one clue only on which to start her search – the name 'Sampford' written in Thomas's diary.

Emma read and re-read the scribbled entry in Thomas's diary. Sampford. Just that one word. Where, oh where, had she heard it before? A frown wrinkled her smooth, pale forehead as she dredged through her memory. It was there somewhere, she was sure: buried deep in the past.

(Flashback now begins in pluperfect tense).

She had just arrived at Turin House, a bewildered, frightened 10 year old, clutching her aunt's hand so tightly that a spasm of pain and annoyance had crossed Aunt Dorothea's face. 'Let go, child,' she had ordered. 'Come and meet your cousin.'

At 13, Thomas was already tall and exceptionally handsome, with an imperious manner far beyond his years, and Emma had accepted her position as his adoring slave almost from that moment.

(Now slip back into past perfect tense – remaining in pluperfect would become tedious – until flashback is about to end).

'You may put your things on that shelf, if you wish,' Thomas said, loftily, greeting her with a magnanimous sweep of his hand. 'This used to be the nursery but it's my den, now. It can be yours, too, if you like.'

Emma eyed him uncertainly. 'Thank you, Thomas,' she answered, at last, in a small voice that struggled to keep a childish wobble out of it. 'I should like that very much.' She lifted her chin and stared warily up at him through misty violet eyes until, rewarded and reassured by his smile, she allowed herself to relax.

(Signal end of flashback by reverting to pluperfect.)

She had never forgotten that first meeting with Thomas. It had remained indelibly printed upon her memory ever since and would remain so until the day she died. Since then, she had wanted no other friend, no other playmate and, as she had grown into adulthood, had wanted to be no man's wife but Thomas's.

(Now we return to main part of story, using the past perfect.)

But now, looking again at that one word so hastily written into his diary, hope suddenly surged through her. She

41

remembered. Sampford was the name of a place Thomas had spoken of with great affection, once, long ago. That was where she would find Thomas, she was now certain. She turned, thrust the diary into her reticule and, with quick, determined steps, hurried from the room. She would set out, that very afternoon, to look for him.

PACE

Pace is closely linked with tension and action and it is essential to vary it or the reader will become bored. For instance, the action of the story must not rush on at breakneck speed without allowing the reader a breathing space, every so often, to ponder on what has been happening, to let it sink in. If it does, it's likely s/he will lose interest. This is where a descriptive passage, or one of exposition, of explanation, comes into its own: it slows the story down a little. A student of mine had a scene in which there was an explosion, trapping an old man and his dog in the building. Within the space of a few paragraphs, the hero had heard the explosion, fought his way into the building, tried in vain to rescue the old man and brought out his body. It was all over far too quickly, not allowing time for the reader to assimilate the significance of what was taking place – or to feel much emotion. The author had not 'milked' the incident of all its potential and, consequently, had lost the chance of increasing the tension. Would the hero be able to rescue the old man in time? Would he, himself, be injured in the falling debris? Would there be a second explosion before he got out of the building?

Conversely, of course, it's necessary to make sure the reader doesn't nod off to sleep because the pace is too leisurely. Partly due to the influence of television, the average modern reader demands plenty of action and dialogue in fiction, all of which increases its pace.

Select words to alter pace

The use of sharp, staccato words such as drag, hit, shot,

burst, thrust, rasp, make the narrative appear to be moving faster, just as longer, softer-sounding words like sauntered, strolled, meandered, slow it down. Naturally, the vocabulary you use will also add to the atmosphere you are creating.

Whenever your characters are in a state of conflict, that, too, will hurry the story along. But the secret is to alternate action with description and/or exposition, though the amount of either will vary, according to the tale unfolding.

Bring in a man with a gun

If you sense the pace of your story is slackening too much, you can always increase it by, metaphorically, using Raymond Chandler's advice: 'If the plot flags, bring in a man with a gun.' In other words, introduce some action. But remember, too, Flaubert's warning that ' . . . action must develop itself. Everything must grow freely and you must do no forcing in one direction or another.'

Another piece of advice from Diane Pearson (a Senior Editor and superb novelist) is that, whenever a story is sagging, introducing dialogue will bring it to life.

Perhaps getting the pace right is partly a question of instinct but becoming aware of it in the fiction of successful authors, by studying how they control it, can help you put it into practice in your own writing. Finally, always ask yourself: does this scene move the story forward? If the answer is 'No' – cut it.

IMMEDIACY

Immediacy is one of those not easily definable ingredients in a story which, nevertheless, must be present. It can make the difference between rejection and acceptance. Because the story and the characters almost leap off the page, the reader thinks he is *there*.

This can only be achieved by a thorough knowledge of the background – so, however well you may think you know it, in order to make the reader feel he *is* actually present, you must first steep yourself in the period of history, the country, the society and so on. Research your background thoroughly before you start writing.

Margaret Thomson Davis, in *The Making of a Novelist*, says that what the writer is aiming for '. . . is to make the printed page disappear, to draw the reader away from the surface of the page he is reading, to join, in the world of his imagination, the character he is reading about.'

SEX

Sex scenes (as opposed to love scenes) can be especially tricky for the beginner writer, largely because s/he may feel inhibited about putting down on paper physical, erotic descriptions. (What will Aunt Mary think?)

There is also an erroneous belief that all novels, in order to be successful, must have 'spicy' scenes. This seems to have arisen because many bestselling novels do contain them and these often seem to have been injected, deliberately, in order to titillate the reader.

Doubtless, there are cases where it has been decided to add what often border on pornographic scenes in the belief that they will improve the book's commercial value. But, surely, no writer of integrity would agree or do so?

The important question to ask, when considering whether or not to include 'sex' in your book, is: is it an integral part of the story – or is it merely intended to shock or titillate?

Today's romantic novels no longer need to stop at the bedroom door and often contain very sensuous and erotic passages. But most authors of the genre give the same advice: if you don't feel comfortable writing them, leave them out. If you have to force yourself to write such scenes, they will come across as being artificial and contrived. That same advice should be applied to all types of fiction.

SYMBOLISM

In fiction, symbolism is a sort of shorthand. John Steinbeck defined it as being a kind of psychological sign language used to 'illuminate and illustrate the whole'. We tend to use symbols in our everyday lives. Choose gaudy colours, say a bright red dress, and you are making a statement: This is me; take notice. If we wear grey or other neutrals, the chances are we don't want to draw too much attention to ourselves. Also, certain colours have come to have particular associations: white with innocence or purity; yellow with cowardice; green with jealousy, and so on.

Objects, too, have symbolic associations in our minds and in our fiction. A house represents security. I was amazed, recently, to discover just how many novels have the word 'house' in their titles, suggesting its importance in their themes. Mountains suggest obstacles to be overcome. Red roses, as we all know, represent true love. A ring or circle stands for perfection or perpetuity; blood for life (or death); an egg for fertility; a key for knowledge.

Weather can often be used symbolically. Gathering storm clouds can suggest a coming emotional storm. Cleverly, at the end of the film of E.M. Forster's *A Passage to India*, the raindrops beating against the window were coloured red, foretelling the blood-letting in Partition's holocaust.

Whichever symbol you use, it will only have significance in relation to the theme of your particular story, helping to point it up. In one of mine, the main character was a little charwoman who had long dreamed of owning a fur coat. Unexpectedly, she had the chance of acquiring one (it had been given to a rummage sale) but there were obstacles preventing her from getting it. I didn't realise until much later that, by having her toiling up a steep hill, every morning, to reach the house where she worked and showing, in flashback, how she'd once climbed the stone steps to the top of the church tower, also on top of the hill, I had been symbolising her ability and determination to overcome difficulties. The fur coat, too, was a symbol because, to this woman, possessing it signified becoming someone of importance, being looked up to instead of being treated as an inferior – which was how she perceived herself at the start of the story.

It may be that we sometimes bring symbols into our writing without realising it. However, I think we neglect a powerful tool if we don't also consciously make use of them, whenever and wherever appropriate.

STYLE

'. . . if any man wish to write a clear style, let him be first clear in his thoughts . . .'

Goethe

At a writers' conference, some time ago, I took part in a discussion in which we attempted to define style. By the end, it was generally agreed that it was almost indefinable. It seems to be a personal way of writing that develops naturally and mostly by instinct, conveying what you want to say accurately and *in your own voice*.

We have to find a style with which we feel comfortable, one that reflects our own personality. If we impose one, artificially, on our writing, it is likely to be stilted – and poor. However that is not to say that analytically reading the work of writers we admire won't influence us in developing our own. After all, painters have always studied the masters in order to learn from them so that 'in the style of' is a phrase used without condemnation. Indeed, Aristotle is reputed to have said that imitation is the beginning of art. However, we should never attempt to write as past authors have done but should rather write in the manner of our own period.

Sinclair Lewis, lecturing to a university creative writing class, said: 'Style is the manner in which a person expresses what he feels. It is dependent on two things: his ability to feel, and his possession, through reading or conversation, of a vocabulary adequate to express his feeling.'

Adjusting style

Another point to bear in mind is that there may be times when you need to adjust your style to fit the dictates of the intended market. For instance, if you are writing for teenagers or, say, a particular magazine, the language and the way you structure it will have to be tailored to meet those specific needs.

Here, let me remind you that a simple style is best. Nothing annoys me more, when reading a work of fiction, than to find it littered with obscure words which I have to keep looking up in a dictionary, thus disrupting my involvement in the story. Sometimes, too, there is an obvious attempt to be 'literary' which merely becomes intrusive (one can easily fall into that trap). Avoid, too, complex sentence-structures which force the reader to go back to the beginning to get the sense of it. Aim for a smooth, pleasing-to-the-ear, as much as to the eye, way of saying what you mean.

Guidelines

It would be impertinent to attempt to lay down hard and fast rules but there are certain guidelines which are generally accepted as being worth following. These are covered here, together with a few of my own.

- It is best not to sprinkle your writing with adjectives. These have their uses but too many of them will over-decorate your prose. Georges Simenon, in a *Paris Review* interview, told of how of how he was once given a very useful piece of advice by fellow writer, Colette (literary editor of *Le Matin*, at the time). She told him his writing was 'too literary, always too literary', and that he should cut out adjectives, adverbs and 'every word there just to make an effect'. You might like to take Mark Twain's advice: 'When you catch an adjective, kill it.'
- Wherever possible, use a strong verb instead of relying on an adverb to qualify a weaker one. For example: 'He complained' is better than: He said, complainingly.

47

- Avoid starting sentences too often with a present participle: Running up to him, she flung her arms around him. It is usually better to write: She ran up to him and flung her arms around him.
- Use the active voice rather than the passive which tends to weaken a piece of writing. Instead of: He was stunned by Libby's action, write: Libby's action stunned him.
- Watch out for over-frequent use of certain words – a trap most of us can fall into. Three I catch myself constantly using are: just, suddenly and almost.
- Beware of starting sentences with: As; Then; Just then; Because. Frequently, they warn of slack writing and 'telling', as in: Just then, Libby appeared and he was stunned by her unexpected behaviour. *Show* him being stunned, as explained in the *Show, Don't Tell* section.
- Use sentences and paragraphs of different lengths to give variety to your prose. Add emphasis, where appropriate, by letting a single word stand alone or by using two or three-word sentences, even if, strictly speaking, they cannot be called sentences because there is no verb. For example: And very glad.
- Sharpen your writing, at times, by starting a sentence with a preposition. (Fling out of the window that pedantic rule you learned at school that you should *never* do so.) Today, this is not only permissible but often to be desired as it helps shorten an otherwise lengthy sentence, at the same time attracting the reader's attention to the point you are making. For example: But Mary would not leave.
- Do not over-load your work with allusions to classical literature, music or painting, or with obscure words or foreign words and phrases. If the reader knows of them already, s/he may feel s/he is being patronised. If s/he does not, you will have made him or her feel ignorant and s/he will not thank you for it.
- Never use clichés or hackneyed phrases. Always find a fresh, original way of expressing yourself. As George Orwell put it: 'A newly-invented metaphor assists thought by evoking visual images.' A modern writer who is a superb exponent of the metaphor, in my opinion, is Ruth Rendell. Phrases such as:

'A voice like clattering dustbin lids.'
'A voice full of crushed ice.'
'Her frown was like the bunching of a piece of creamy velvet.'
'The river winding through its thin sleeve of willows.'
What word picture those brief descriptions conjure up! But, a word or two of warning: these are examples taken from another writer's work so, whatever you do, don't use them in your own.

DRUMMING UP IDEAS

Tutors of creative writing often hear the plaintive cry: Where do ideas come from? Well – where *do* they come from?

Turgenev once said: 'All through my career as a writer, I have never taken *ideas* but always *characters* for my starting-point.' Henry James talked about ' . . . the precious particle . . . the stray suggestion, the wandering word, the vague echo, at a touch of which the novelist's imagination winces as at the prick of some sharp point.' Doesn't that really say it all? Ideas are all around us: in a snippet of overheard dialogue, a newspaper report, an anecdote related to us by an acquaintance, any one of these can be enough to start the imagination working overtime. Flaubert was given the idea for *Madame Bovary* by a friend, Louis Bouillet, who told him of a certain incident which had occurred, locally.

The much admired P.D. James has said that for her, invariably, a particular setting will spark off a novel, while Somerset Maugham once commented that he would never live long enough to be able to use up all the ideas he had for stories. He went on to say, in *The Summing Up*, that 'In one way or another, I have used in my writings whatever has happened to me in the course of my life.' In other words, his own experiences provided him with ideas. Milan Kundera puts it more poetically: 'The novelist destroys the house of his life and uses its stones to build the house of his novel.'

The seed from which a novel or short story springs might well be some unresolved conflict in your own life which you need to work through in fictionalised form. Or perhaps you have a strong conviction that something is morally wrong (racism, sexism, working/housing conditions) and you want to expose it, as did Charles Dickens.

Have you ever looked at a painting and begun to wonder about the people in it? A favourite of mine is by the Victorian painter, Atkinson Grimshaw, in which a young woman is walking alongside the wall surrounding a big house. It's a moonlit night and there isn't another soul around. Who is she? What is she doing there, all alone? A dozen and one stories spring into my mind whenever I see that picture. Is it the young lady of the house who has been keeping a lover's tryst? Or is it a maid returning from her day off? So far, I haven't worked up any of these ideas into a story but I'm sure I will, one day. But I don't mind anyone else taking it because I am sure that if I set a group of twelve students to write on the same topic each one would produce a totally different piece.

However, not all ideas are strong enough to sustain a novel and may only be suitable for a short story. Test this out by asking yourself: is your idea about someone in conflict with society (in which case you probably have material for a novel), or is that character only concerned with a personal crisis which, once resolved, will end his dilemma? If the latter, then almost certainly the right vehicle will be a short story.

Once you start opening your eyes and ears, you will find ideas in plenty.

THEME

Although every piece of fiction will have a theme, remember that it is not the writer's job to preach. You need to get over your 'message' much more subtly than that. Try to open your reader's eyes and mind, help him understand some aspect of human nature a little better, throw a different light on it for him through your characters' actions and reactions.

Gustave Flaubert, in his *Intimate Notebook*, wrote: 'If you begin your book telling yourself: it must prove this or that, the reader must come away from it religious or ungodly or erotic – you will write a bad book, because in composing it you have offended against truth, distorted the facts.'

Judith Krantz has said that she writes '. . . about the same things all storytellers have concentrated on . . . money, power and love. These are at the heart of storytelling, always have been.'

This is hardly surprising, is it, because are they not the three strongest drives throughout human nature? It seems to me that, while the basic themes of most bestselling fiction are woven around these three, they can be broken down into sub-categories:

- Survival
- Rejection
- Being misunderstood
- Betrayal
- Death of a loved one (including an animal).

Take a close look at some successful novels and note the basic theme and other subsidiary emotive ones.

So far as a short story is concerned, its theme can often be expressed in an aphorism. For example: faint heart never won fair lady; virtue hath its own reward; he who gives shall receive. Whenever you read a novel or a short story, try to identify the theme and see how the writer wove his or her story around it.

PLOTTING

Around the turn of this century, a Frenchman named Georges Polti devised a list of all the possible plots available to the writer. These have become known as the Thirty-Six Dramatic Situations. Unfortunately, because of copyright protection (the date of his death is unknown and there are also translation rights existing), it is not possible to reproduce this list here. However, it is available in book form (see Useful Publications).

In fact, it would seem likely that a Venetian writer, by the name of Gozzi (creator of Turandot upon which Puccini's opera of the same name was based), was the originator of these situations. Indeed, Polti talks of rediscovering them. Goethe and Schiller, too, pondered on the possibility that there was a finite number of plots. But Polti can be given credit for writing them down in such a form that they have not been lost to future generations.

As we have already seen, any one scenario involving any number of characters can produce as many different plots. Polti posits that, although there are only these 36 dramatic situations, each can be combined with one, or more, other to produce different plots. Each of these 'situations' results from conflict between 'two principal directions of effort' or two opposing forces. Each situation, too, can be subtly altered by the degree of opposition or intent by the characters involved and by the 'degree of consciousness, of free-will and knowledge of the real end toward which they are moving.'

Although the language of the book is somewhat archaic, it isn't too difficult to recognise some of the 'situations' in well-known literature. For example, the tenth situation, Abduction, has often been the basis of popular fiction, over the years (starting with a rich sheikh whisking a woman away to his desert stronghold and making her fall in love with him). Recently, the modern phenomenon of 'tug of love' children and their frequent kidnapping has spawned a spate of books and films. The tale of Turandot, the Eastern princess who set her suitors riddles which they must either solve or be put to death, is clearly based on situation number 11: The Enigma.

Every serious writer, I believe, is bound to be interested in these Dramatic Situations, and the book certainly makes for interesting reading.

CHECKLIST OF ESSENTIAL ELEMENTS IN FICTION (THOUGH NOT NECESSARILY IN ORDER OF IMPORTANCE)

- Plot
- Conflict
- Background
- Setting
- Characterisation
- Dialogue
- Theme
- Tone/atmosphere
- Suspense/tension
- Reader identification
- Pace
- Emotion
- Symbolism
- Motivation
- Use of five senses
- Viewpoint
- Indirect exposition (show, don't tell)
- Flashback
- Structure/shape
- Immediacy

The novel

' . . . every novelist has something in common with a
spy: he watches, he overhears, he seeks motives and
analyses character, and in his attempt to serve literature he is unscrupulous.'
Graham Greene, WAYS OF ESCAPE

Although many novelists start by writing short stories, not
all do so. None the less, the latter provide an excellent way
of understanding the need for shape and structure in
writing and also for putting fictional techniques into practice. Also, being shorter in length and quicker to write, less
time and emotional energy is risked, thus softening, somewhat, the blow of a rejection. While still hard to take, it is not
quite so devastating as when 80,000 words or more, repres-
enting perhaps years of your life, keep thudding on to your
doormat with depressing regularity.

WHAT EXACTLY IS A NOVEL?

The French word for it is 'roman' which gives a clue to its
original meaning: a medieval tale from the early French or
Provençal in which were described the adventures of a
chivalrous hero. Clearly, the romantic novel has evolved
from this.

The novel, as we know it, today, made its appearance
around the beginning of the 18th century, although students of literature consider that Cervantes' *Don Quixote*
(1612) helped shape it more than any other work. The first
English novel of note is generally regarded as being *Pamela*

(1740) by Samuel Richardson (who, incidentally, did not become a novelist until he was 50).

Walter Allen, writer, critic and one-time editor of the *New Statesman*, suggests that the novelist deals '. . . with men in a specific place at a specific time . . . ' Allen believes that the English novelist, often without knowing it, has been greatly influenced by Shakespeare and that, so long as he is performed and read, his influence will continue.

We can say that a novel is a work of fiction, a fact attested to by the note often found at the front of it: 'The characters and situations in this book are entirely imaginary and bear no relation to any real person or actual happening.' This does not mean that the incident or character from which the idea for the book germinated never happened or existed or that the book itself does not reflect life today, as observed by the author. Everything has to begin somewhere. But real life, however dramatic, obviously is not, in itself, fiction.

Truth *can* be stranger than fiction. The latter must have shape or form, whereas life – as most of us discover only too often – is an unpredictable shambles. Perhaps, then, we could say that the modern novel deals with real-life happenings in an unreal way; P.D. James has described it as being a 'rearrangement of reality'.

What do we mean by reality? Colin Wilson, in *The Craft of the Novel*, suggests that: 'Reality is *not* what happens to be the most real to us at the moment. It is what we perceive in our moments of greatest intensity. And the peculiar power of the imagination enables us to cling on to this vision after the intensity has vanished.'

The novel deals with man in relation to society rather than merely to himself. It is about *people*, not concepts. For example, it may be about a man whose potato crop has failed and whose family, therefore, faces famine, but will not be about a bad potato crop; about the effect upon a woman (or women) of a particular war, not about war in general. It is the personal crisis set against the backcloth of society, the world in which those people happen to be living at that moment in time, and it will deal with several moments of truth.

THE QUESTION OF LENGTH

There is a saying in the literary world that a story should find its own length. This is undoubtedly true but, if you aspire to seeing your book in print, you would be wise to ensure that it conforms to an acceptably-publishable length. An *average* novel, today, is around 80,000 words, though a 'blockbuster' may be 300,000 words long. But, to attempt the latter before you are a fairly accomplished novelist and without its having been commissioned would be a tremendous act of faith. It might pay off, but the odds would be against it – with the likelihood that you would become so disheartened by the rejections after so much hard work that you would give up writing forever. Far better to lower your sights (but not the standard of your writing) until you've had at least one book published.

THE DIFFERENT KINDS OF NOVELS

Basically, there are two types: 'main-stream' or 'mid-list' and 'category' or 'genre'. While you are still learning your craft, you would be wise to concentrate on the latter because, in today's market-orientated world, they increase your chances of success.

Time and again, publishers and literary agents advise would-be novelists to write books that can be slotted into a definite category, simply because it makes them easier to sell. Once you have a track record, you may be able to interest a publisher in a 'mid-list' book. I say 'may' because I know of one author with a string of books to her credit who sent out her last one 14 times before it was finally accepted.

Again, you might be the exception that proves the rule. You might have written a brilliant book that is snapped up by the first editor who sees it. Fine – stick to your guns if you believe in yourself and your book – but be prepared for the possibility that you might meet with rejection after rejection. It might not even necessarily be an intrinsically bad novel: it might just be that, from an unknown author, it is not considered marketable (that is, not profitable).

Let me emphasise that we live in a commercial world. As writers, we are in the business of producing books, just as publishers and bookshops are in the business of selling them. We may not like to think of them as being mere commodities but that is what they are. While we may, at this stage of our career, write in our spare time and so not depend on it in order to live, those others would starve if they could not sell their wares. It's as well, whenever you feel embittered about having your work turned down, yet again, to ponder on that. It helps put it in perspective, I think. And, after all, isn't it rather a 'chicken and egg' situation? We are also readers and buyers of books and the kind we choose, ourselves, must influence what finds its way on to the library and bookshop shelves.

It is not my role to dictate to you what you should write, only to offer advice on the assumption that you are reading this because your aim is to sell your work. Therefore, there follows a brief description of each of the main categories into which by far the majority of published novels fit. Every year, others do appear but, if you can direct your first book into one of these, you will improve your chances of success. If you are not sure into which particular slot or genre your writing might fit, then spend a little time in one of the bigger bookshops or libraries, looking at the different sections – which are usually clearly marked. Then buy or borrow one or two that seem of a similar type to your own. Make a note of the publisher, read them critically and analytically.

- Pay attention to the length (overall, and of chapters).
- Who are the Main Characters?
- Is the story told from one viewpoint or several?
- Look at the language and style (refer back to Section One).

This will give you a general guideline, a map to help you find your way through your chosen literary minefield. Some publishers and magazines that take serials have tip-sheets or guidelines available on request (if you enclose a stamped, addressed envelope).

Once you have done this basic research, you will have a much clearer idea about which genre is the right one for you, be it a family saga, contemporary romance, spy thriller or whatever. You will know, also, roughly the overall number of words required, the average length of each chapter and will have ear-marked a possible publisher or two.

Contemporary Romance

These vary in length from around 45,000 words to 85,000, depending upon publisher and degree of sophistication. The developing love relationship between hero and heroine is always central to the plot (they are, after all, romances). Generally speaking, the hero is older than the heroine, more worldly-wise and probably wealthier.

Heroines should reflect today's modern young women who no longer play a submissive role in society, nor are necessarily in subordinate-type employment. They can, and often do, have careers as pilots, deep-sea divers, architects, stage-directors and so on. Such backgrounds (unless familiar to the author) must be thoroughly researched, as must the foreign and exotic settings so often used. However, romantic UK settings such as the Highlands of Scotland, Devon or Cornwall, are just as acceptable.

These stories are mostly told in the third person – from the heroine's viewpoint – but, on occasions, will go into that of the hero. Danielle Steel is a popular and prolific American author of the contemporary romance which also has a wide readership in the US.

Historical Romance

These are usually longer than the contemporary romances – at about 85,000 plus words. Again, the love-interest is central to the story. The background must be historically accurate, though the Main Characters (hero and heroine) will be fictitious. Katherine Woodiwiss is a popular American author of this genre.

Historical

The background must be historically accurate and well-researched and, while the minor characters will be fictitious, the Main Characters will often be people who have actually lived. Although this genre is currently out of fashion, the advice of a senior editor of one of the largest international publishing houses is to 'hang in there' because, from her many years in the business, she has observed there are always cyclical patterns in reading. Nigel Tranter, Elizabeth Byrd and Dorothy Dunnett are superb writers in this genre.

Period

These, generally, are from Regency times up to, and including, the First World War. As always, thorough research is essential in order to bring the period to life. Catherine Cookson, Margaret Thomson Davis and Jessica Stirling are authors who spring to mind, here.

Spy Thriller

The ending of the Cold War and the tearing down of the Berlin Wall have destroyed the favoured *milieu* for this type of novel. Le Carré, and anyone attempting to emulate him, will have to find another setting or invent an imaginary one. I mention this to warn against continuing in this vein: it is very definitely *passé*, now. Other successful authors of this genre, whose books are worth studying, include Helen MacInnes and Evelyn Anthony.

Whodunnit

This genre remains perennially popular. Length can be from 75,000-90,000. Agatha Christie's novels are reputed to be outselling the Bard himself, with those involving her elderly female sleuth, Miss Jane Marple, more popular than Hercule Poirot. If we also consider P.D. James' extremely popular books with their Commander Adam Dalgleish and Ruth Rendell's with Chief Inspector Wexford, all these translate well on to the small screen, achieving high ratings and, doubtless, a small fortune for their authors, not to mention an ever-increasing readership.

Going further back to that master of the genre, Raymond Chandler, we can find a common denominator: they all have a likeable 'tec with human frailties and personal problems. It seems, therefore, that a detective story, in order to be popular, must obey certain 'rules'. It must have a detective with whom the reader can sympathise and, to a certain extent, identify – and it should produce a dead body within the first few pages.

Raymond Chandler, in his famous essay *The Simple Art of Murder*, describes the hero of a detective story thus: 'He must be . . . a man of honour, by instinct . . . He might seduce a duchess but would not spoil a virgin. He will be a relatively poor man who will not take money dishonestly. He is also a lonely but proud man.' Chandler suggests, too, that 'down these mean streets a man must go who is not himself mean . . . ' and that 'He talks as the man of his age talks, that is, with rude wit, a lively sense of the grotesque, a disgust for sham, and a contempt for pettiness.' Chandler ends, 'The story of this man's adventure in search of a hidden truth would be no adventure if it did not happen to a man fit for adventure.'

Although it seems certain that whodunnits will remain popular, it is of no use creating a Philip Marlowe, Chief Inspector Wexford or Miss Marple look-alike. Your hero/heroine must be of today's world and not a pale imitation of one of the classic literary detectives. If you choose this genre you will need to create a totally original type of detective as Ellis Peters did with Brother Cadfael in her brilliant, eponymous Chronicles set in medieval Shrewsbury, a setting which provides that 'plus' factor previously mentioned. Make sure, also, that your character has qualities suggested by Raymond Chandler:

- S/he must have the common touch
- Must be incorruptible by money or favour (though s/he can be, and probably is, tempted, at times)
- Must have courage in the face of danger

- Must also be human enough to feel pity and to fall in love, however unwillingly.

Psychological Thriller

Ruth Rendell's *A Demon In My View* is a superb example of this genre in which the author goes into the twisted mind of the Main Character but in such a way that we cannot help but feel a sympathy for him. It is the workings of the *mind* that are the focus for this type of novel.

Horror

The 'horror' novel takes advantage of our desire to be shocked and frightened, even though we pretend we don't actually want to be. Yet it must still seem to be within the bounds of what we think just *could* be reality. Stephen King is probably the best-known author of this type of novel. Ramsey Campbell is another author worth studying and it is understood that publishers are currently looking for new, good novels in this genre.

Science Fiction/Fantasy

The boundary between these two genres is so blurred that I have linked them, here. They continue to be extremely popular but, although their settings may well be futuristic, and will certainly be outside the bounds of reality as we know it, their characters must still have the same conflicts and emotions as ordinary humans have, today. They must still struggle for power or money or love; fight evil, suffer and, finally, the protagonists must overcome all obstacles.

Because the background will be one with which the reader may not be familiar, you must describe it in sufficient detail (though *not* through large chunks of narrative) so that s/he is able to 'see' it clearly. Certainly, you must know this imaginary territory thoroughly. You should know the mores of your created world, its laws, its governmental and societal structures, its language, its likely enemies and dangers. Remember, you are asking the reader to suspend disbelief, so your story must be credible.

Doyen of science fiction, Isaac Asimov, in his guidelines for writers for his eponymous magazine, emphasises the need for stories to involve change, growth or development in the characters' lives.

Isaac Asimov, Anne McCaffrey and Terry Pratchett are popular authors of this type of novel.

Westerns

J.T. Edson is probably the best-known exponent, here, although this type of fiction has been rather out of favour, in recent years. According to one leading literary agent, however, it is due to make a come-back but, as always, an accurately-described background is essential.

Gothics

This genre has been out of favour in the UK for a considerable period of time, though gothics still sell in the US. Victoria Holt is probably one of the best-known authors. Invariably told in the first person, always with a brooding house for a setting. Jane Eyre could well be considered to be the prototype.

Romantic Suspense

Mary Stewart and American author, Phyllis Whitney, are masters (or mistresses) of the genre. Similarly, it has been out of favour, for some time, with UK publishing houses – although Phyllis Whitney is a best-selling author in the US. However, according to one reputable source, anyone producing a really first-class work of this kind would soon find a publisher. Invariably told in the first person because that creates the most immediacy: you are *there*, experiencing everything alongside the narrator.

Sagas

A saga is a big book, often a 'blockbuster' of some 200,000-300,000 words. It may span several generations of one family and, because of its complexity, needs careful pre-planning; otherwise you (and the reader) are likely to get lost in a maze of characters, situations and dates. Sometimes, they are set around a world-wide event such as a war or a national disaster.

The fact that a saga is about the lives and loves of several characters means there is plenty of scope for *conflict*. You will need one or two really nasty or downright evil characters to be pitted against your hero and heroine, as well as numerous dire circumstances and situations for them to struggle against.

You can also introduce people who actually lived during this period, thus adding verisimilitude to the story. Naturally, you must research thoroughly to ensure accuracy and that these people could actually have been where you've put them and done the things you've had them do.

Because of the large cast in a saga, it is wise to write a brief biography for each member (in more depth for your hero and heroine) to guard against renaming them by mistake or spelling the name differently (as in Jenny or Jennie) or changing the colour of their hair or eyes halfway through. Make them sufficiently different from each other to avoid confusing the reader.

Autobiographical Novels

It is generally said that most (though certainly not all) first novels are autobiographical. In fact, *all* fiction draws upon the author's experiences, to some degree. We all know what it is like to feel the whole gamut of emotions – pain, anger, guilt, sorrow, envy, jealousy, hurt, love, fear and so on. Therefore, although we may never have actually murdered anyone, in all probability, at some time in our lives we have felt an anger so intense, so frightening, that we quickly got it under control before we did any real harm. And there can be few of us who, as a child, never once stole something, however small – some sweets, a penny, a coveted object that belonged to another – and if we dig down deep we can recall the fear of being caught, as well as the guilt.

By using all of these fragments of memories we create the stories that will hold our readers' interest and, hopefully, will remain with them for long afterwards. Indeed, I once heard someone say, 'Memorable writing can happen only out of memorable living.'

A second premise worth reiterating is that Emotion is the foundation stone of all good fiction. It is the springboard from which your characters launch themselves into their story: what motivates them to take the actions that constitute the plot. (A simple definition of plot is 'characters in action, attempting to achieve a goal or solve a problem'.)

An autobiographical novel, therefore, can be said to stem from the author's unforgettable and deeply-emotional experiences. Maybe this is why Pearl Buck said that no one should attempt to write a novel before they are 40 years old. In other words, until they have *lived*.

This kind of writing has advantages and disadvantages. Conjuring up from your past should enable you to depict vividly certain scenes; to jerk the heartstrings of your reader. But you can only do this if you can rid yourself of inhibitions about exposing yourself, how you think, how you feel about large and small issues; how you perceive the truth. It may take more courage (whether in the fictionalised form of a novel or an actual autobiography) than pure fiction. It is, however, likely to be more successful if you can manage it. Perhaps this is why, so often, first novels are highly successful while subsequent ones are not nearly so well received.

A few very brave novelists actually state that a particular book is an autobiographical novel as Somerset Maugham did with *Of Human Bondage*, which helped exorcise some of the inner pain he had suffered as a child. He dipped his hand into the well of experience and wrote about the truth as he saw it.

Many popular autobiographies have resulted from authors depicting their lives (sometimes serious parts of it) in a light-hearted, humorous vein. Betty McDonald's *The Egg and I* and *The Plague and I* (the latter about her brush with TB); James Herriot's 'vet' books; Lilian Beckwith's set in the Hebrides (*The Sea For Breakfast* once had me laughing out loud in a hotel lounge). However, humour is partly subjective and isn't something anyone can consciously set out to write. You either can do it or you can't. If you can make people laugh, or even smile, you have a rare gift which, together with carefully-honed craftsmanship, could produce considerable rewards.

WRITING TO A FORMULA

Before we move on to planning your novel, let's consider a word often associated with category novels – formula. What does it mean? And are novels written to a 'formula' likely to be less good than those that are not?

One well-known New York literary agent, writing on this topic, countered with another question. Did the Brontes, R.L. Stevenson, Balzac, Conrad, Tolstoy and other writers of the past write formula fiction? He then gave two answers: They certainly did! They most assuredly did not! He illuminated this apparently paradoxical reply by suggesting that, if we analyse what is going on below the surface of classic novels, we find the same genre 'formulas' and 'tricks of the trade'. Most bestselling fiction has certain elements in common (check it out for yourself): a sympathetic hero or heroine confronting a challenge, facing conflict, thwarted by obstacles and overcoming them to achieve happiness, victory, wealth, glory, love, peace of mind.

PLANNING

To have got this far, you probably have at least a germ of an idea for a plot in mind and one or more interesting characters springing to life. Now, you are ready to start planning in some detail.

Here, again, I am only offering advice. Many successful authors do scarcely any pre-planning at all. Others, like

Rosemary Sutcliffe, know their beginning, roughly where they are going and a few developments along the way. Many more, like Iris Murdoch, do a great deal of pre-planning. Indeed, she has said: 'I invent the whole thing in enormous detail before I start writing at all. That can take longer than writing.' Irving Wallace, too, author of the bestselling novel *The Prize*, says: 'The planned or outlined novel has in its favour the virtue of being creatively thought out, worked out, disciplined in the author's mind and on paper, with the major characters getting their due, with the main stories and subplots being told in proper perspective and balance . . .'

You will eventually find *your* own way – whichever feels right for you. However, I believe that, until such time as you have your first work published, you would be wise to spend some time drawing yourself a metaphorical map, even if you deviate from it as your book progresses.

Have you, for instance, a gripping opening, one that will introduce the reader to your Main Character and make him/her want to find out what happens next? Can you 'see' some of the high points along the way – those strong emotional scenes of conflict? Do you know how the story will end? Jot down some notes NOW. Later on, should you reach a stage where your imagination seems to have dried up and you are seized by the dreaded writer's block, you will at least have some signposts to get you back on to the right path before, in despair, you abandon it completely.

WRITER'S BLOCK

Phyllis Whitney, the highly-successful American author of romantic suspense previously mentioned, has written one of the most practical and helpful books ever on fiction-writing – *Guide to Fiction Writing*. In it, she describes how she overcame this frightening drying-up stage, with which she was usually beset at around chapter three or four. She has developed a comprehensive note-book system with various sections in which she scribbles down ideas as they occur to her, however random and perfunctory, for the plot, characters and background. Then, whenever creative paralysis occurs, she reads through her notes, and her inspiration is rekindled.

What I particularly like about this book is that Phyllis Whitney never dictates. She only offers advice which, from her own long experience, she has found works both for herself and others. She has been there, too! She knows how painful rejection after rejection can be; she knows how frightening writer's block is. And I can vouch for its effectiveness, too. (For more on writer's block, see Section Four.)

SEQUENCE OF WRITING

Another point to consider is whether to write your novel chronologically, that is, starting at the beginning (even though you may well change this, later) and work through till the end or to write major scenes as and when you 'see' them in your mind. This is a matter of choice; we are all individuals and must find the way that suits us best. Some writers insist that the latter method is totally wrong, because the characters will change as the novel progresses and you get to know them better, but I don't think anyone should be so didactic about how any individual approaches his work. For myself, to 'see' a scene in my head as vividly as watching it unfold on a screen and not to at least rough it out on paper seems crazy. I'd be too afraid of 'losing' it or of its powerful images diminishing.

For instance, suppose you know that, at some point in your novel, there will be a major episode in which the heroine will be confronted with someone from her past. lover, mother or child, perhaps. You feel sure this traumatic meeting is going to take place outdoors, on a wild and windy heath, maybe. If this scene begins to grow, to come to life in your imagination until you feel you simply have to write it, then do so; you will be able to weave it into the story at the appropriate place, later.

STRUCTURE

In a novel, high points are carefully placed throughout, rising in a succession of peaks until the climax is reached. Visually, its shape is like a mountain, climbing in a series of mini-summits to the top. Seeing it like this can help you plan your book before you actually start writing. I know that some novelists say they don't plan ahead at all but I suspect the vast majority of us need a rough guide for the journey we're undertaking so that we can find our bearings if and when we get lost. And writing a novel is like a journey – a journey to the truth. When we make any kind of long trip, we usually begin by making a list of things to take with us, so let's start considering some of those we will need for this one.

- Main Character(s).
- Setting/background.
- Period in time – contemporary, period or further back in history – and likely time-span covered.
- Basic situation: that is, what the Main Character is striving for.
- Possible obstacles in his/her path – who, or what, will be opposing him.
- Secondary characters.
- The theme: what the story is about, what it is saying. If you aren't sure, at this stage, don't worry – it will become clear, later.
- Viewpoint – first person; third person singular; third person multi-viewpoint.
- The opening. This may change as you get further into your book but you need to have an idea of where it should begin before you actually start writing. Certainly, it will be close to a *point of change* in the Main Character's life.
- Will there by any sub-plots?
- Type of novel – 'category' or 'mid-list'?
- Which publishers might you aim at and what length?

Now I propose we examine the above points in more depth.

CHARACTER

Although some novelists say that setting is the point of
conception for them, I believe that it is almost impossible to
separate character, setting and situation when a story is
being created in your mind; there is an unconscious process
of osmosis in which all three fuse virtually simultaneously.
Therefore, almost certainly, we know who our main character will be before we even put pen to paper.

Many novelists say that, as the novel progresses, they
sometimes find a minor character taking over, assuming
more and more importance in the story, so that they have to
re-think and even start again with this other character as the
main one. But whoever is first 'on stage', almost invariably,
will be the protagonist, even though you may decide to tell
the story from a variety of viewpoints throughout.

To help get to know your characters, writing a mini-
biography for each of the major ones, at least, is often
advocated. Even if you've based them, loosely, on someone
you know or have known, you can't possibly know them
completely, because you don't have access to their thoughts
or feelings, as you do in the case of those you have created
entirely out of your imagination. You need to know as much
about them as about yourself. Here, I will give a list of things
about them which you might like to complete, apart from
the more obvious points such as age, sex, date of birth and
so on which we have already dealt with in Section One.

* Attitudes to: marriage, divorce, children, education, old
  people.
* Reaction to: dishonesty, breaking of vows, stealing, quar-
  relling, trust, acceptance of gifts or help.
* Effect of early memories of: death of, or separation from,
  a parent, sibling, beloved animal; rejection; not being
  believed/being mistrusted.
* Likes and dislikes.
* Taste in: music, painting, books, theatre.
* Hobbies: sport, travel, collecting – whether antiques of
  any kind or, say, modern editions.
* Career/profession: why was that one chosen?

• Ambitions: what, if any, are they? What reason for them?

Add to this list any other points you can think of which will help you build up a detailed portrait of your character(s), so that you become on such intimate terms with them that you'll know, instinctively, how they will react in any situation in which they find themselves.

SETTING

You will make life easier for yourself if you choose a setting or locale that you know reasonably well or, at least, have visited. Otherwise, use an imaginary one. Often, in romantic novels, exotic locations are used because they add to the escapist element and, obviously, it is unlikely their authors will have actually been there, themselves. But they will have done the essential preliminary research!

One golden rule applies here: whichever setting you choose, it should be because this particular story could not have taken place anywhere else. For example, *Gone With the Wind* could only have been written against the background of the American Civil War. And could Thomas Hardy have set *Far From the Madding Crowd* anywhere else but in that area of Dorset he called Wessex? Or M.M. Kaye have set *The Far Pavilions* anywhere but 19th-century India? It will also be either because you have a deep personal knowledge of the terrain and its people or because you have researched it *thoroughly* – and possibly both.

BACKGROUND

Again, using a background with which you are familiar will help cut down some of your preliminary work. For instance, if your hero is a fighter pilot or your heroine a fashion model and you have been one, yourself, or know someone who is, that will help you give your book the necessary 'ring of truth'. Even so, you will probably have to do some research because it is so easy to get small details wrong –

particularly if it is a long time since you were in that situation – and the chances are that some of your readers will spot such errors.

Most published writers carry out a considerable amount of research to ensure an authentic background against which their Main Characters act out their particular stories.

PERIOD IN TIME

Unless you have a special interest in a particular period in history, you will probably choose to write a contemporary novel. If you are attracted to bygone days, you will need to research thoroughly to ensure you get the small details correct. These are what give the flavour of the times far more than the big events.

List the major happenings of the period to ensure no mistakes creep into your book. For instance, that you don't have your heroine travelling by train/coach/plane when that particular mode of transport had not yet reached the place where she is living.

Remember, too, that cataclysmic events will have an effect on your character(s).

Names are probably even more important in a period novel because they must be ones that would have been used, then. Speech, too, must reflect the times; guard against anachronisms, like putting words into the mouths of your characters that were not in use, during that time in history.

TIME-SPAN

You will probably have an idea of the length of time the book will cover, from the opening scene to the closing one. This does not, of course, take in any flashbacks you may use. There is no arbitrary rule, here. Some novels span several generations (family sagas) while one of my favourites takes place during a single afternoon – Nina Bawden's *Afternoon of a Good Woman*.

CHARACTER'S GOAL

The vast majority of novels are about someone desperately wanting something, striving to obtain or attain it and being prevented from doing so (at least temporarily) by obstacles of various kinds and of varying intensity. (This doesn't have to be something concrete like amassing a fortune – it can be abstract like wanting success in a particular field or restoring one's good name.) If you can define this, even if only in your own mind, right at the beginning, it will give you a focal-point – a goal to work towards, along with your main character. At the end of the story, s/he will usually have reached his/her goal (though, possibly, only to find it has lost its significance), in the 'category' novel, at least.

OBSTACLES IN CHARACTER'S PATH

These are the metaphorical boulders with which you strew your character's path to prevent him/her from solving the problems and achieving goals too soon. They are part and parcel of the conflicts you will set up throughout the novel. However, they must arise out of each other, *causally*, and not separately with no connection to each other. Think of the children's rhyme: For want of a nail, the shoe was lost. For want of a shoe, the horse was lost. For want of a horse, the battle was lost. As each obstacle or complication is overcome, another rises up to take its place.

Think about any possible conflicts and complications you could introduce. What is there in the relationships between your characters (and, in particular, your main ones) that could be the source of a major conflict?

THEME

Every story must have a theme, an implicit message of some kind, otherwise it is not worth the telling. Nancy Hale, in *The Realities of Fiction*, says: ' . . . the illusion of life is best rendered when it is supported, just as real lives are, by a framework of purpose which, in the novel, is called theme.' Frequently, it is about a writer's obsession. The main character in Somerset Maugham's *Of Human Bondage* (which he called an autobiographical novel) was lame but the story was really about Maugham's own disability, his stammer. It was his re-arrangement of reality. And Christopher Isherwood has said that 'Every writer has certain subjects that they write about again and again and . . . most people's books are just variations on certain themes.'

Because of the writer's close personal involvement in the theme, he will be more able to bring to it that vital ingredient we've already discussed – emotion. But never forget that it is not the novelist's task to preach.

By the end of any piece of fiction, the theme should have been proved, otherwise the reader will feel dissatisfied. Even in a contemporary romance, which we know will have a 'happy ending', there will still be an underlying theme: True love can overcome mistrust of the opposite sex, for instance, or revenge is bitter, not sweet.

VIEWPOINT

In this context, the only decision you have to make is whether to tell your story in the first person singular (the 'I' as narrator) or in the third person. If the latter, you can tell it from one character's angle only or, as is most common, from that of several – multiple viewpoint. If you choose third person narration, you will probably also use the omniscient viewpoint, at times, when scene setting. We've already taken a look at the pros and cons of selecting viewpoint, in Section One. Now the choice is yours to decide which one seems right for your story.

BEGINNING

Deciding on the right place in which to open your novel is not always easy. Wherever you begin, however, get the story moving *quickly*. If you don't, the publisher's reader will probably only skim through a few paragraphs and, if it hasn't grabbed his or her attention by then, is likely to add it to the rejects pile.

Always begin at a point where you can involve your readers with your Main Character immediately. Make them feel they simply have to know more about him/her. Let them know, right away, who the Main Character is and where and when the action is taking place.

Study a number of published novels to see how and where they open. Usually, a particular situation sets the whole drama of the story in motion, triggering off the series of complications and conflicts until the final resolution. The following are some typical basic situations that have been used to open well-known novels:

- An event occurs, beyond the control of the Main Character, which brings about a major change in his/her life. For instance, in *Gone With the Wind*, it is the American Civil War that forces change in Scarlett O'Hara's life and sets in motion everything that follows. The event might be the death/ruin of a father/guardian, leaving the heroine penniless and alone (as in *Jane Eyre*). Or it might be the arrival of a stranger with subsequent consequences for the inhabitants of a town or household (*Wuthering Heights* used this basic situation).
- The Main Character is struggling against the environment, in some way. Man/woman overcoming all odds to achieve fame and fortune is a universally popular plot which many writers have used to bring themselves success, for example: Barbara Taylor Bradford's *A Woman of Substance* and Jeffrey Archer's *Kane & Abel*.
- The Main Character is involved in a moral fight, perhaps against injustice or racial prejudice, as in *To Kill A Mocking Bird*.

The opening of your novel should immediately set the tone, indicate if it is to be serious, humorous, romantic, a thriller or mystery. Almost always, it will be a point of change in the Main Character's life. It will present a believable, larger-than-life (and, usually, sympathetic) character in an interesting situation and in a colourful setting, facing some conflict which is linked to the theme of the story.

The first page

The first page of your MS is of vital importance. Think about how you, yourself, choose a book either in a shop or library. Whatever makes you pick it up, initially, don't you always then skim read the first page? And, if it doesn't grab your interest, immediately, don't you usually put it down and try another? So, put yourself in the shoes of the editor lifting your MS out of that 'slush' pile and make sure that his or her attention is caught right away.

To help you give your own first page that necessary impact, analyse the openings of successful novels to try and see how their authors achieved it. Ask the following questions:

- Did the Main Character and the situation in which he/she was placed intrigue enough to make you want to read on?
- Did it set the tone of book right away: that is, was it clearly a romance, a mystery, adventure, horror and so on?
- Did it inform as to the who, where and when?
- Did it immediately begin to set up the tensions and conflicts of the novel, hinting that trouble lay ahead?
- Did it, perhaps, begin with an event outside of the Main Character's control which is about to set in motion a sequence of events that will change his/her destiny?

The following is the opening from A *Woman of Cairo* by Noel Barber, which illustrates something of the above.

'Life seemed so wonderful to all of us in those happy days in Cairo. I wonder sometimes whether the splendour of Egypt blinded us to the real facts of life, in much the same way as the servile smile of an Arab anxious to sell a scarab to a British Tommy masked a hatred of the foreign oppressor. But then Cairo was a city of intrigue which cast a spell over all of us.'

In just three sentences, we know where (Cairo) and roughly when (the mention of a British Tommy suggests it's just before the last war): we learn who the narrator is. We know the lives of the main characters are about to be dramatically changed and the implication is that it will be by something completely beyond their control.

Studying how bestselling authors plunge us straight into their stories should help us learn a few more of those 'tricks of the trade' which, in the end, will help lead to the acceptance of our work instead of rejection.

ENDINGS

Almost as important as a story's beginning is its ending. As Mickey Spillane once said: 'The first page sells a (mystery) novel and the last page sells the next one.' It is well to remember, too, that publishers are not interested in one-book authors. A first novel almost invariably makes a loss, but they hope to break even with a second and make a profit with a third. I know one writer whose publisher is refusing to bring out the paperback edition of her first novel until she has produced the manuscript of her second.

Never forget that readers hope and expect to put a book down with a feeling of satisfaction that it could only have ended the way it did. One way it should *never* end is with the Main Character awakening from a deep sleep or coma or coming round from the anaesthetic after an operation and discovering that everything that happened had been but a dream.

In all fiction, there is the 'obligatory scene', the climax of the story, which is immediately followed by the resolution. Even in a novel that is left open-ended for the reader to make up his own mind about it, if the writer has done a good job, that ending will still seem to be the right one. In *Gone With the Wind*, for instance, each reader will interpret it according to his or her own personality. This was a novel about, above all, survival. Survival was all that mattered to Scarlett O'Hara from the moment she was embroiled in the American Civil War until Rhett Butler walked out on her.

Those final sentences must be some of the best known in the world of books: 'I'll think of it all tomorrow, at Tara. I can stand it then. Tomorrow, I'll think of some way to get him back. After all, tomorrow is another day.'

Did Margaret Mitchell intend to write a sequel, I wonder? Any writer who wants to should always leave the reader with a distinct feeling that, if he is patient, he will learn yet more about the doings of the Main Character – and that famous ending certainly leaves one with that impression.

BRIDGING OR TRANSITIONAL SCENES

Today's novels do not always have (or need) a bridging or transitional scene, one that links one period of time with another, one place with another. However, if they are omitted, you must ensure that the reader is not confused. Leaving a double double-space or putting in a row of asterisks to indicate a break in time or place will prepare the reader for this – or you can start another chapter (or section, if chapters aren't used). But it is probably best to give a clue at the end of the previous scene as to what the next will be about. For example, Evelyn Anthony, in *The Poellenberg Inheritance*, finishes one section with:

'All right,' he said again. 'It's a bargain. Next stop Paris.'

She begins the following section with:

'Well,' Dunston said, 'so you're off to Paris. Lucky you.'

You can always use the simple stylistic device of a short piece of narrative, such as is used in *To Kill A Mocking Bird* by Harper Lee: 'The remainder of my schooldays were no more auspicious than the first.' This gets through several uneventful years which were of no importance to the development of the story.

Or: By the time the sun had sunk below the horizon, James was 50 miles away. And safe. At least, that was what he had told himself. He wasn't quite so sure when he awoke, the following morning, to find his door wide open and a stranger standing just inside the room, watching him.

As it wasn't necessary to know about James's actual flight from one point to the next, a few lines of narrative are sufficient to get him from A to B so that the reader knows exactly where he is when the next piece of action begins.

SUB-PLOTS

Longer novels, particularly sagas, usually have one or more sub-plots. These add a richness to the texture of the main story. For example: the main plot hinges on the battle of an illegitimate son of a wealthy landowner, at the end of the 19th century, to be accepted and claimed as his son and heir. But there is a cousin who considers he is the rightful heir. While the bastard son is the Main Character, a strong sub-plot could be developed around the cousin and his life and endeavours. There might even be another, told partly in flashback, of the elicit relationship between the Main Character's mother and his landowning father, a relationship that is either ongoing or starts up again.

ANALYSING NOVELS

To try to understand what makes one novel a bestseller and another come winging back, time and again, with a rejection slip, it can only be of benefit to analyse those which, by common consent, have been successful – and which, more importantly, *you* have enjoyed.

Artists of every kind, throughout the ages, have studied the masters to learn about technique – and writers are no different. And, although Somerset Maugham once said, with legendary ascerbic wit: 'There are three rules for writing the novel. Unfortunately, no one knows what they are!' – he also offered some sound advice. He suggested that the best way to learn craftsmanship in novel-writing was by studying the craftsmanship of successful novelists.

If you've ever tried to read, critically, a book which has 'hooked' you from the start, you will know how difficult this is. However, even if it diminishes your pleasure, you will reap the rewards, later. Or you can re-read it, the second time asking yourself specific questions to discover what made you choose it from the host of others available.

- Was it because of the author? If so, what is the quality of his/her books that makes you enjoy them?
- Was it, perhaps, the title that caught your eye?
- Whatever persuaded you to pick it up initially, almost certainly, you will have glanced at the first page, and possibly the next two or three. Was it, then, something about the Main Character (who will have been mentioned in the opening paragraph) that intrigued you? Was it the setting? Or the situation into which it appeared the Main Character was about to be thrust? Or was it, perhaps, the style of writing?
- Was the suspense, the tension, kept up throughout the book so that you couldn't bear to put it down because you simply had to find out what happened next?
- Did you quickly become involved with the hero/heroine and his/her problems?
- Did you like the descriptive passages or did you find yourself skimming over them because they held up the action of the book, perhaps?

Note your answers carefully because in them could lie the success or failure of your own book. But, however much you liked the entire story and however much you try to put what you've learned into practice with your own, remember: the first three pages are the most important of the whole book. On them will probably depend its fate when it arrives in the publisher's office. Those few pages are the ones that will determine whether the reader proceeds to a complete reading.

Time spent on writing and re-writing the opening to your book will be time well spent. Every successful novelist I've ever met emphasises that.

SUMMING UP

Now that we've gone through the essential elements that make a successful book, here is a checklist to keep you on the path to success:

- Until you have at least one published novel to your credit, aim at a specific category to increase your chances of success.
- Analyse novels you've enjoyed to try to see why you did.
- Pay particular attention to the first three pages, but don't do less than your best for the rest.
- Give your book a 'plus' factor (something to make it stand out from the rest of the 'slush' pile).
- Make sure it has that page-turning quality by increasing the tension and creating suspense at every opportunity.
- Give it immediacy so the reader has the feeling he is actually *there*.
- Ensure you have created sympathetic, believable characters.
- Write the sort of book you, yourself, like to read. Immodestly, Disraeli said: 'Whenever I want to read a book, I write one.'
- Give your book an ending that will leave the reader feeling satisfied – and making a mental note to look out for your next.

Check List for Common Mistakes

When you have finished your novel (or as you work on it) it is worth going through the following list to check you haven't made any of the most common mistakes.

- Is the pace uneven? Is there too much action without slowing down from time to time, to allow more reflective passages? Are there *longueurs* where you have over-long descriptions which carry no real weight? Are there long passages of exposition so there is the danger the reader might become bored?

- Is your style too 'flowery' with too many adjectives? Have you been over-liberal with adverbs? Are your sentences too long and unwieldy? This is where it is particularly important to know the readership you are aiming at.
- Is there enough dialogue?
- Is there too much 'telling' and not enough 'showing'?
- Are your characters depicted in sufficient depth?
- Is the plot too contrived, not developing naturally from the characters involved?

YOU'VE FINISHED YOUR NOVEL, NOW WHAT?

Your book is finished, revised and re-written till it is the very best you can make it; it's neatly typed ready to send out, so what do you do, next? By now, you should already have an idea of which publishers might be suitable – but do you send the entire typescript, part of it or maybe just a preliminary query letter? If you are wise, you'll take the latter course. It has several advantages:

- It will only cost you the price of a couple of stamps (one for a self-addressed envelope).
- It will elicit a much quicker reply, which is why most publishers prefer this approach rather than being inundated with large parcels containing several hundred pages. And, even if the reply is negative, it's better than waiting in uncertainty for weeks or even months.
- If you wish, you could write to two or three companies, simultaneously.

Keep your letter as brief as possible and to the point. It should give the gist of the plot in a couple of paragraphs and tell a little about yourself, your background, successes to-date and writing ambitions (publishers are not interested in one-book authors). And it is sensible to address it to a specific editor, if possible. Check out the name of the Senior Fiction Editor by phoning the switchboard operator at the publishers you have in mind. Here is an example of a Query Letter:

Dear . . .
I have just completed my first novel (although I have had over 20/several short stories published in national magazines). It is 100,000 words long and, I believe, would fit into the 'family saga' category.

Briefly, it spans three generations of a farming family in Somerset, starting in the late 19th century and finishing in 1950. The main thrust of the story hinges on the feud that began in 1897 over who was the rightful heir to the then prosperous farm. The conflict is resolved, finally, when the grandson of one branch falls in love with the granddaughter of the other. There are two sub-plots involving other members of the family.

I am familiar with this particular background and setting, having spent my childhood on a farm in the region. I have already begun work on a sequel which will bring the story up to the present day.

If you think it might be suitable for your list (*if writing to an agent*: if you would be interested in handling my book), I should be happy to send you the entire typescript. Meantime, I enclose a stamped addressed envelope for your convenience.

Yours sincerely,

Having spoken to a number of publishers and agents, it seems that they all prefer a letter, in the first instance. A word of warning: *never* send a copy of your book to both a publisher and a literary agent, at the same time. And, if you decide to send part of your book, *never* choose random pages but always the first two or three chapters, plus a synopsis.

If, having tried a number of publishers without success, you decide to try an agent, always tell him/her which of the former have already seen it.

As regards sending out several copies of the book at the same time, while this is a fairly acceptable practice in the US, it is still rather frowned upon in the UK.

Synopsis

Many would-be writers find the idea of producing a synopsis somewhat daunting. They needn't – because it is really only outlining the novel so that a potential publisher can see at a glance what it is about. If you are submitting your first book, including a synopsis will be helpful to an editor. If it is a second one which you hope will be commissioned, an editor will want to see a fairly detailed synopsis, first, though a writer is never expected to stick to it rigidly.

For your first novel, however, a synopsis should not be more than a couple of double-spaced pages. It is helpful to break it down into chapters, provided there are not more than, say, 12, outlining the main action of each in a couple of sentences. For example:

Chapter One   The heroine, Holly Manton, learns she has inherited an Italian villa so long as she agrees to live there for six months of each year. She goes to Milan to make a decision and meets the hero, Toni Brazzi, discovering that he is the other beneficiary of her uncle's will, though she doesn't know why.

Chapter Two   Initially, Holly is attracted to Toni but an odd and frightening 'accident' occurs which makes her believe he resents her presence and is trying to make her leave.

Chapter Three   The local contessa throws a masked ball, to which Holly is invited. She recognises Toni, escorting a very beautiful woman, and overhears a conversation that heightens her suspicions.

(*The rest of the synopsis continues in the same way.*)

WHAT ARE PUBLISHERS LOOKING FOR?

The market for books changes constantly but publishers, and literary agents, also, do attempt to predict future trends.

One of the larger, old-established agents told me that he foresees the return of the Agatha-Christie-type detective story and of straightforward, police-procedural crime novels. He suggested also there might soon be a renewed interest in the Western.

Another well-known agent, Carol Smith, said that everyone is seeking 'good stories about people you care about'. She is looking for a fresh voice with a fresh view of life. She does *not* want imitators of Catherine Cookson or other well-known authors. She strongly advocates writing about what you know and finished by saying that a good writer enables the reader to 'look through a window at somebody else's life'. She also said that, although they are still fairly popular, she thinks the market has just about been saturated with the 'family saga'. One 'don't' Carol Smith mentioned in particular was that 'horror' mentioned earlier: author intrusion. Another personal one is letters that contain old-fashioned and pompous words such as 'peruse', which bode ill for the enclosed manuscript.

She suggested that a minimum length for a saleable novel today (apart from certain genres such as the contemporary romance for specific publishers) is around 80,000-100,000 words; a Whodunnit could perhaps be slightly less, say, 75,000, especially for a first novel.

Finally, Carol Smith advised every writer to believe in him or herself. And, if your book is turned down by one publisher, send it out again, immediately.

The short story

'I saw the short story as a narrative of a single event, material or spiritual . . .'

Somerset Maugham THE SUMMING UP

DEFINING THE SHORT STORY

What exactly is a short story? Is it merely a question of length? There have been many attempts to define or describe it. Nancy Hale, in *The Realities of Fiction*, compares it with a precision watch, while the novel, she suggests, is more like the workings of a juggernaut. Thinking in terms of analogies, I see the short story as taking a day trip somewhere when there is no time to deviate from your destination. The novel, on the other hand, is more akin to a fortnight's holiday during which you can wander off the main route to admire the scenery, visit other places of interest, if you so desire. You might also liken the short story to a delicate watercolour or miniature rather than the vast sprawling canvas in oils of the novel.

My own prosaic definition is this: it is a short piece of fiction concerned with the vitally-important problem or goal of one character only. After overcoming various obstacles or complications, the resolution will be brought about by that character's own efforts, by which time he will also have undergone an emotional or spiritual change.

How long is a short story? Put simplistically, it should find its own length. For instance, one with a twist in the tail will probably be no longer than 1500 words, with 500 being the minimum. At the other end of the scale, 10,000 words is likely to be the maximum, though there are few markets for this length. As with any other kind of writing, you need to study your market because it is of no use sending one of this length to a magazine that only takes those of up to 3,500 words.

The BBC's Radio 4 Short Story slot needs about 2,250 words, while the more 'literary' magazines and some national competitions (including the Ian St James Award) look for anything up to 10,000 words. As a rough guide, though, a length of 2,500-3,500 is a good one for the majority of women's magazines, which constitute by far the main outlet.

What is a Short Story About?

The short story is always concerned with a small *but significant* incident in the life of the Main Character. It will involve his solving a problem or achieving a goal *of great importance* whether material, emotional or spiritual. For example:

* To find a suitable dress to wear at son's wedding in order not to let him down in front of his fiancée's wealthy relations and friends.
* To impress new mother-in-law with housekeeping skills.
* To come to terms with death of a loved one.

The resulting conflict will usually be stronger if either it is between close friends or relatives or between two people of different background, culture, needs and desires.

The Fiction Editor of a well-known 'glossy' magazine has said that: 'A living story should give the reader a new understanding of nature, of human problems. It should stab the spirit awake.' Maren Elwood, in *Characters Make Your Story*, says: 'The successful story . . . is one in which people react characteristically to situation and to opposition, to love and to hate, to pleasure and to pain.'

Structure

We've all heard the saying that a good story should have a

beginning, a middle and an end and, while you are still learning, it is wise to keep that in mind. Save experimentation for later, when you have successes behind you.

The other 'rule' is to observe at least two of the three Greek Unities. These originated from Greek drama – which had the same tight structure now associated with the modern short story:

- **Time** Greek drama usually covered a period of 24 hours. For the purposes of the short story, it is advisable to use a short time-span – anything from one hour to, say, a week. A longer period (not including flashbacks) would tend to weaken it.
- **Place** If a story opens in someone's garden, for example, and it ends in the garden, the Unity of Place would have been observed. However, this is the Unity most often ignored without detriment to the story.
- **Action** This, in effect, means that the story is told from one viewpoint only throughout its length – that of the Main Character. The only reason for not adhering to this is when, *after careful thought*, you have decided your story will be improved by not so doing.

Before we go on to break a story down into the three sections mentioned, a word of warning about one particular type of structure to avoid: the 'story within a frame'. Beginner-writers often fall into this trap, perhaps because they remember those stories of years ago in which one character, often sitting round an inn fire, would relate an experience that had happened to a friend. These are totally out of fashion, now, and unlikely to find a market.

Beginning This should:

- Introduce the Main Character.
- Set the tone (horror, romantic, humorous, human-interest and so on).
- Set the scene.
- Show the Main Character's problem or goal.

87

Middle   This section should show the motivation for the Main Character's subsequent actions. In it, we should see the Main Character striving to solve his problem but only making things worse as complication piles on complication until the climax, the 'blackest moment', is reached. This should come about logically because of everything that has occurred up to that point. It should also contain within it the seed of the dénouement, the resolution of the initial problem.

End   This should bring the story to a close in a way that leaves the reader satisfied. It should never be the result of a coincidence but always because of the Main Character's own efforts. It should be swift and not drag on into an anti-climax. For example, if the widow has finally come to terms with her husband's death, the story should not go on to explain how she spends the next few years of her life.

If possible, it should have kept the reader guessing as to the outcome right up to the end, by which point the Main Character should have changed his/her attitude, in some way.

Now, let's examine the actual process of writing a story, step by step.

PROCESS OF STORY-WRITING

Once you have an *idea* for a story (and an idea is not a plot) there are certain questions you need to ask before you can go any further.

- Whose story is it? This may seem obvious but, frequently, it is not. This is because the same scenario, involving more than one character, can be written from the viewpoint of each and every one of them, resulting in as many different stories.

  To find out whose story it is (or should be) a good test is to ask yourself from which character you could wrest the most emotion. (I'll illustrate this in a moment).

- What is the Main Character's real problem or goal? Again, this may seem obvious but, often enough, the actual problem or goal is masked by a superficial one.

The importance of answering these two questions correctly, while at the planning stage, is illustrated by the following example – a story once submitted to me for criticism.

In brief, it is about a man who suffered a heart attack through over-work and involved his wife and his son, this obviously causing them great distress. It ends with the man coming home from hospital and offering temporarily to look after a dog whose owner had died, thus providing him with an incentive for exercise and something to fill his now-empty days.

Because the writer had not, first of all, decided who the Main Character was (whose story it was), it constantly shifted viewpoint. It opened with the sick man's, moved to the wife's, then to the son's, back to the man's and so on. And, because the writer had failed to answer that question, neither had he identified the real problem.

As the story progressed, I realised that, in fact, it was the wife's story and her problem. The flaw in her character was that she had been overly ambitious for her husband and overly houseproud in wanting a beautiful house that wasn't truly a home. Her husband had always wanted a dog but she had resisted that, fearing the mess it would make. It took her husband's near-fatal illness to make her see the futility of ambition and pride. So, instead of the coincidence of being asked to take care of a dog, for a few weeks, she should have 'come to realise' how wrong she had been and gone out to find one to give her husband as a pet. She would then be rewarded by seeing the pleasure on her husband's face and his healthy flush after he and the dog returned from their first walk together.

The writer had thought his story was about a man who has a heart attack, whose wife and son are worried about him and who will be able to accept not going back to work if he has a dog as a companion for a while. By making it the wife's story, it becomes much stronger because it is really she who needs to change her attitude to life. Of course, it could still be written from the man's viewpoint, in which case he, too, would have to alter his views about work, but that would be a totally different story and probably for a different market, not a women's magazine.

• What is the tone of the story – what type will it be – romantic, humorous, human-interest and so on?

Only when you have answered all three questions to your own satisfaction are you ready to begin writing.

Beginning

Where should your story open? The advice often given to beginner writers is to chop off the first third of the narrative and that will probably be about the right place. This is because too much background explanation is often given, at the start, which merely holds up the story proper. If it is necessary for the reader to know this, it can be fed in, later, perhaps by means of brief flashbacks.

Always plunge straight in, mid-stream, close to a crisis point that forces your Main Character to make a decision. This will introduce the vital ingredient, *conflict*, immediately.

A line of dialogue often makes an effective opening: 'Get the hell out of here, Tom Dickinson. This is *my* patch!'

Equally, a piece of action is a good way to begin: Debbie slammed the door behind her as she ran from the room. That was it. She'd had as much as she could take!

Another way to start is with an intriguing statement: The first time Mr Johnson saw it, the sun was shining. The second time, though, the heath was shrouded with mist and he almost missed it.

However you open your story, you must 'hook' your reader immediately so that he wants to know *what happens next*. In each of the three examples above, I think the reader would be sufficiently interested to want to learn more.

Middle

You now need to ask more questions – the 'what ifs' and 'suppose thats' – in order to plan the logical series of crises, each one worse than the one before, which culminates in the climax and brings about the resolution.

Let's use the example of the woman afraid of letting her son down at his wedding. Ostensibly, her problem is how to buy an expensive and elegant dress to wear on the occasion. In reality, however, it goes much deeper: she needs to 'come to realise' she will be loved and liked for herself, not for her appearance. The theme, then, can be summed up as 'Clothes do not make the man' and this must be proved by the end.

But: *what if* she's been saving up till she has just enough to buy a new dress, shoes and a handbag – and then learns her closest friend desperately needs the money to visit her dying daughter in Australia? Another crisis point – another desperate moment of decision.

Remember that it is through your characters' actions that we get to know them. Therefore, if she commiserates but decides her own need is greater, she will go down in our estimation; we will lose sympathy with her. If, though, she struggles with her conscience and then uses her savings to buy an airline ticket for her friend, our sympathy will grow, which is what you want.

But now what? She really is in a mess, isn't she? So how is she going to get out of it? Another question: *suppose that* she scours the charity shops and manages to find a dress that was once extremely fashionable, having belonged to one of the wealthy ladies of the town? And *what if*, when she arrives at the church/reception, she realises the bride's mother (or other guest) had been the voluntary helper who had served her in the shop and has recognised her? It's too late for her to rush home and change and, in any case, she hadn't anything else remotely suitable to wear. What is she going to do?

I'm not going to suggest any further crisis points or what the climax might be in case too many magazine editors find themselves inundated with similar stories! In any case, the number of crises will depend on the type of story and its length. But it will need a strong *climax*, one that will force the Main Character into a final decision which will result in her learning something about herself, about life and about other people.

Ending

With this particular storyline, she must 'come to realise' that she need not have worried. She should have trusted that she had imbued her son with the right values and that he had chosen a wife with the same ones. Whatever her outward apparel, her new daughter-in-law will greet her warmly and her son let her know he is proud to be her son.

Thus you have a satisfactory ending. There is no need to continue, explaining how she chatted to guests after the couple left for their honeymoon and found she got on famously with the bride's mother. That would constitute an anti-climax which should always be avoided.

Often, a point of reconciliation between the Main Character and another produces a good ending. One you must *never* have (as has already been stated) is that resulting from a coincidence: the Main Character must always solve his own problem. For example, you cannot have your Main Character adrift on the ocean in a terrible storm with his boat about to capsize when a second one appears round the headland and rescues him, just in the nick of time. This might happen in real life: it must not in fiction.

I hope you now see the importance of asking questions *before* you start the actual writing of your story. Time spent thinking through and planning it, first, will be time well spent.

CHECKLIST

Always check your short story against these points before deciding it is complete and ready to send off to a publisher.

- Have you identified whose story it really is – that is, the character about whom the reader will feel most strongly?

- Have you identified the Main Character's true problem or goal?
- Have you introduced the Main Character immediately?
- Does the story open at a crisis point and quickly establish the Main Character's problem or goal?
- Have you shown the motivation for his subsequent actions?
- Have you established the theme – that is, what the story is about?
- Have you planned a logical series of crises which move the story progressively forward, culminating in the Climax, the 'blackest moment' for the Main Character?
- Have you observed at least two out of the three Unities?
- Have you cut out any minor characters who are not absolutely necessary to the story?
- Is the ending a satisfactory one with the Main Character solving his/her own problem and having changed in attitude by the end?
- Have you added those 'brush-strokes' that will make your story stand out from others on the editor's desk?
- Have you given your story an eye-catching, relevant title – if possible, one that encapsulates the theme?

MARKETING SHORT STORIES

Some women's magazines will not accept unsolicited stories, in which case, somewhere on the inside cover, usually, there will be printed a notice to this effect. However, many do. All of those published by the D C Thomson group, situated in Dundee, not only welcome short stories but also offer positive encouragement and advice to any writer who shows promise. Payment may not be as high as with other markets but it is more important to achieve even small successes, at the beginning, in order to build up self-confidence.

Spend some time, each week, browsing along the magazine racks in one of the larger newsagents, to decide which particular magazine you feel you would like to write for and then buy several issues to study in depth and really get to know the kind of stories the editor likes and what is an acceptable length. This is much more likely to be productive than looking at a number of different markets, at the same time.

As already mentioned, there are also numerous competitions for short stories held throughout the year, and advice on how to find out about these is given on page 131. Also, anthologies of new writings seem to be becoming increasingly popular and these are worth looking out for. While it is very unlikely that any publisher would be interested in bringing out a collection of stories by any one unknown writer, you might like to set your sights on having one story published in such an anthology.

'Confession' or 'True-Life' Story

Markets for these were once prolific but, of recent times, several have either disappeared completely or no longer accept unsolicited material. However, the magazine world is constantly changing so it pays to keep an eye on the situation.

These stories have a specific structure which relies heavily on the use of flashback and often hinge upon a flaw in the Main Character. By the end of the story, s/he will have learned a lesson, possibly losing what they had most wanted through their own folly or may have pulled back from behaving badly just in time.

For example, suppose a young married woman was feeling neglected because all her husband seemed to think about was his job. She might be tempted to have an affair to prove to herself, at least, that she was still attractive and desirable. This story could end two ways. She could discover that her husband was putting in many extra hours at his work in order to pay for the exotic holiday she'd always wanted, making up for the fact that they hadn't been able to afford a proper honeymoon. She could 'come to realise' her husband's worth before she actually started the affair. Or, she could learn the truth too late: she could lose the husband she really loved and discover, also, that her lover wasn't interested in a serious commitment.

94

Again, because of the wide variety of stories used, and the different age-groups at which they are aimed (teenagers, young unmarrieds/marrieds, and so on) it is up to you to carefully study the market before attempting to write for a specific magazine.

Twist in the Tail Story

These never seem to fall out of favour with editors, providing they are well-written with a truly surprising ending. They are usually no longer than about 1500 words.

The main reason for lack of success is that there has been a failure to plant clues throughout the story. Thus the ending, although a surprise, is not seen as being inevitable. The reader should be able to put the story down, thinking: of course, I should have guessed!

One piece of vital information should always be held back until just before the end. If you can give your story a double, or even triple, twist, it will increase its chances of success.

O. Henry and Roald Dahl are the two names that spring to mind when thinking of this type of fiction. Perhaps the former's most famous story is *The Gift of the Magi*. In this, an impoverished young couple each sell their most precious possession in order to buy the other the desired Christmas present. The young husband sells his watch to buy tortoiseshell combs to adorn his wife's glorious hair and she sells her hair to buy him a chain for his watch. The theme of love being worth any sacrifice is pointed up even more by the story having a Christmas setting.

The best twist-ending stories are those that have a theme and are firmly based on character. However, the twist *is* the story and so must be thought of first and the story, in effect, plotted backwards.

The Radio Story

The main outlet for radio stories in the UK is the BBC's Radio 4 Short Story slot. These last for just under 15 minutes and should be between 2,100 and 2,300 words long.

The sound of words and rhythm of sentences is especially important with stories intended for the ear. Those told in the first person (the 'I' viewpoint) are particularly effective because of the intimacy of the medium. You, the narrator, are confiding your experiences to one other person, sitting alone in his or her kitchen, car, sitting room.

Include occasional, oblique repetition of any vital bit of information in case the listener has missed that particular point because, of course, he cannot turn back to check.

Although the stories are enormously varied, certain types are not usually accepted (though, as always, there are exceptions to the rule). These are: the purely-romantic, mystery or ghost story (notoriously difficult for the less experienced writer) and twist-endings. The BBC's Short Story Department is looking for stories that entertain and does not want anything too grim. It prefers the general emphasis to be on straightforward narrative, not cluttered with too much dialogue, and with the number of characters kept to a minimum.

While all unsolicited material is looked at carefully, the standard, generally, is found to be so low that the department now relies more and more on stories that have previously been published. The moral here is to make certain that yours are of such a high standard that they *demand* to be broadcast. (Incidentally, the radio story analysed at the end of this section was an unsolicited submission).

They should be sent to the BBC in London (Broadcasting House, London W1A 1WW) unless they have a regional 'flavour', in which case, send them to the appropriate regional office in Scotland, Wales or the Midlands. Expect to have to wait about two months for a verdict.

A selection of broadcast stories will soon be available on cassette from some book shops: worth looking out for in order to study closely. Or you could record some, yourself, and listen to them several times to help you get the 'feel' of what is required and understand why those particular ones were chosen.

ANALYSING CONSTRUCTION

Lewis Hosegood, the author of three novels and with a number of broadcast stories to his credit, has kindly given permission for me to reproduce one of his stories in order to help illustrate the importance of construction. *Homesickness* was broadcast by the BBC as a Morning Story in January, 1985.

The idea sprang from an account in the national newspapers of two young Russian soldiers who had deserted during the Afghanistan war because they were homesick.

HOMESICKNESS
by Lewis Hosegood

It was the photograph of his son Mikhail that finally caused Arkady Dmitrievitch Kuznetsov to break down and weep.

It showed a seven-year-old boy in a woolly bobble hat, holding aloft a glove puppet in the form of a duck, serious-eyed for the moment, that is to say for the purpose of the snapshot in the park, but clearly about to dissolve into merriment. Something, someone behind the camera, had amused him. The small mouth trembled on the point of laughter. And apart from the darkish skin he looked just like his mother.

Arkady had never seen this child. The boy had been born six months after his defection in New York. Indeed he hadn't even been aware then that Irina was pregnant. If he had he might have acted differently.

It had all been so easy. He had merely stepped out of the Opera House, taking his spare violin case packed with the few valuables he possessed, and walked into the nearest Metropolitan Police Bureau. The rest had been long drawn out but ultimately successful. Despite threats and cajoleries he had stood his ground, refused to be interviewed inside the Embassy, and finally they'd given up. After all, he wasn't anyone of any significance. But Arkady had thought otherwise. At forty he'd grown tired of languishing in the back row of the second fiddles with little chance of promotion, despite the ability he knew he had, until someone died or retired. He sought something better.

Now, nearly eight years later and a leading soloist with most orchestras in the USA and in Europe, they had caught up with him. He had received a letter from Irina. The postmark was Nvrodny Krasnoie. It was where they had spent their early married life, before getting a flat in the Moscow suburbs. She was living with her parents.

Arkady took the letter with him into the hotel lavatory for some reason and read it there. There was no need for such secrecy here in Vienna. But perhaps old habits died hard. That was the way he'd used to read Solzhenitsyn.

'Dearest Arkady,' it began, warmly enough – and that shamed him for a start. They had parted on a quarrel.

'News has reached us through Aleksandr that you are well and enjoying success as a concert soloist. I am so glad. It is what you always wanted, isn't it? I think of you constantly. Things are fine here with us all. It has been a nice summer. I have a good office job with the Leninsko Fabryk which has a splendid canteen.

'Little Mikhail is going to school now. I thought you would like this snapshot of him. I haven't included one of myself. I'm afraid I'm no longer so pretty; you would be disappointed. It was taken in Timoshenko Park – have you forgotten it? The trees are so beautiful at this time of year. Do you remember, we used to collect chestnuts by the bagful when we were hard up. But they were so small and tough we couldn't do anything with them, even after boiling! Happy days!

'Mr Beritkhov has been very good to us here. It was he who persuaded the authorities to permit this letter. I have written before, I assure you, but they were all returned 'Address outside limit'. He says he feels certain you would be allowed to return if you applied through the proper channels. It would be lovely to have you back for the New Year. I get very sad sometimes thinking of our student days. They seem so long ago, another life . . . '

Arkady covered his eyes. So – she hadn't remarried then. And little Mikhail, dark like himself, speaking good Russian, bursting to answer in his Primary class, hand straight up like a fir tree – he could see it. And Timoshenko Park in autumn where they'd sat and argued earnestly about everything imaginable. Either there or strolling through the Tretyakov Gallery. What wouldn't he give . . . ?

And then he thought: Wait a minute – if Aleks knew of his whereabouts why hadn't he offered to take the letter out with him on his travels? They all did it.

Arkady went down to the restaurant and bought himself a coffee, Austrian style, black with a glass of water. There he put on his reading glasses and studied the letter again carefully. As far as he could make out it had been posted only a fortnight ago. Considering the fact that it had been forwarded from Paris that was extraordinarily quick.

'Unfortunately we may have to move out of this flat,' it continued, 'since it's not really intended for more than two. Ilya Beritkhov says he knows of a little place, just for me, if I'd go and work for him. Mother and Father might be able to look after him, of course, but – '

'*Dieser Platz ist frei, ja?*' a voice said. Arkady looked up to see a man standing there, his hand on the back of the other chair. He nodded.

The man sat. Still smiling he ordered a beer. When the waitress had gone he rolled himself a cigarette, tidied the end, then paused in the act of lighting it. He held it delicately between two fingers. 'You don't object?' he said, in Russian.

Arkady stared at him.

Exhaling a thin stream of smoke, the newcomer said: 'You would be very welcome back, you know. It's quite true.'

Arkady took off his reading glasses and put the letter away. 'You know about this then?' he said. It was as he thought, the whole thing.

'My dear friend – may I call you that? Mr Kuznetsov is so formal. And Arkady Dmitrievitch is yet a little presumptuous. After all you're quite famous now. One should not be too familiar. But here we are, two compatriots in a foreign city . . . ' He paused to remove a shred of tobacco from his lips. 'Yes, I know about it. It would be stupid to pretend otherwise. I also know about the stupidity of the authorities. We've all had to suffer in our time, haven't we?'

Arkady finished his coffee in cautious silence. The man was fair skinned with golden eyes, like a carp. Who was he? 'They are so clumsy,' the Russian continued. 'I agree with you, my dear fellow. But believe me, you have nothing to fear. We will bypass them.'

'Why should I go back?' Arkady said. Apart from Irina, his heart kept telling him. And little Mikhail. And the Russian sunsets, the wheatfields, the birch trees, café music and wide empty streets. 'I wish to play solo violin.'

'But you would have a guaranteed place at the Conservatoire. With them you could still be a major soloist.'

'Within territorial limits.'

'Well, well, that remains to be seen. It depends.'

'Upon what?'

'It depends on your intelligence, of which you have a great deal. And your sensible co-operation.'

Arkady watched the man help himself to a free newspaper from the rack. 'I suppose they want to make some sort of publicity out of it?' he decided. One more disillusioned runner from the West. The new wave in reverse.

'Not at all. We need your talent. It's as simple as that. Why should it be confined to the devil? Isn't there a saying about him having all the best tunes?' The man wasn't really studying the *Wiener Tageblatt*. He put it down. 'You're too good to waste, that's all,' he said.

'They didn't think so once,' Arkady reminded him.

'I must go.' The man rose. 'Think about it,' he said. 'At least take a return visit. A little holiday. See your wife and son. No problem. It can be arranged.'

'A one-way ticket,' Arkady considered.

'By no means. You have a French passport now. No one can detain you against your wishes. We are not barbarians.' He collected his coat and gloves, put on his hat. 'Think about it, Arkady Dmitrievitch. Sleep on it. Meet me here again at the same time tomorrow.'

Arkady accompanied him to the revolving door. There were so many things he wanted to ask, none of which he could put into words.

Outside on the steps, the night air struck cold. They stood for a moment watching the traffic grinding round the Prinz-Leopold Platz.

'All that questionable display of wealth,' his companion said, pointing. 'What is it? Mm? Compared with love? And Honour? The family, and the esteem of those that matter, the people walking on the pavement who love music and will queue for hours in all weathers to hear it? Oh yes, they love music here too, I know – but they come in their taxis, in their evening wear. Only in Russia will they applaud you also for being Russian. And only we, my friend, know precisely what that means. I suspect . . . Here in the West you can buy a new car every year. Is that really a good exchange? Think about it.'

He was gone.

Arkady walked in the opposite direction, the length of the square. It was beginning to drizzle. The traffic lights gleamed their changing reflections on the cobble-stones. All the vehicles stopped, and people walked. Aimlessly he walked with them. His head full of thoughts, pictures. He saw Irina in the heavy arms of Ilya Beritkhov, little Mikhail being denied a proper education, going to a restricted school for gypsies and second class citizens. He also noticed a street kiosk with a poster on it advertising a concert at the Stadt Musik-Theater, his name in the middle, but that wasn't imagination, it was real, the script Roman.

Was it only a couple of hours ago that he'd been rehearsing there? To come back to the hotel to find the letter awaiting him in his pigeon hole? 'Another life,' she had said.

He stood in front of the poster for a moment contemplating it. Under the rain it had peeled slightly, revealing another beneath. Last week's celebrity had been a well-known pianist. Arkady stood uncertainly in the drizzle meditating. Next week his own name would similarly be hidden, someone else's pasted on top. But love – could that so easily be obliterated?

On the corner of the square, the traffic hurtling again, he took the letter from his pocket to look at Irina's handwriting once more by the light of an overhead street pylon.

When he glanced up, there on the other side of the road he saw a bunch of Viennese waiting to cross. And among them was a woman in a fur hat, holding the hand of a small boy by her side. The child had a darkish skin and was clutching a Muppet toy to his chest.

Arkady drew in his breath. It was like a vision.

It wasn't them, of course; how could it have been? But just for a moment, in his agony, they were real enough. Then the woman, tired of waiting for the lights to change, turned to walk on towards the illuminated fountains around the statue.

'No, wait!' he even heard himself cry out in his confusion. 'Irina, don't go. Don't go!'

At the sound of his voice the woman looked over her shoulder. And it was just as well she did so, for the child, balancing on the kerb, had tripped and stepped off.

Arkady froze in horror. It could all have been so ghastly. But even before the warning blare of the car horn the mother had clutched him back to safety.

He watched them clinging to each other, the woman white faced, the boy waiting for the scolding she was still too shaken to give. Arkady allowed his trapped breath to escape. He was glad he had called out. It might have been them, the boy his.

Somehow, the envelope, falling from his nerveless fingers in the incident, had gone under the wheels of the traffic and now lay in the road, wet, begrimed, and indecipherable. Yet that didn't matter. His name didn't matter. He still held the letter in the other hand.

He turned and made his way back to the hotel.

Analysis

Let's now analyse why this particular story was successful and why it works both on the printed page and on the air. We'll start by dissecting it into the three sections mentioned.

Beginning

- The Main Character is introduced immediately – Arkady Dmitrievitch Kuznetsov. Clearly, with that name he is

Russian and we know, right away, that he is vulnerable and emotional (he weeps at the photo of his son). We also quickly learn that he is a defector to the West and a leading violinist, aged almost 48.

- The tone is set immediately – it is a poignant and human-interest story.
- The setting is Vienna during the Cold War.
- The problem is obviously to do with his small son, whom he has never seen: indeed, he had not even known his wife was pregnant when he defected. The *crisis* that sets the whole story in motion is the letter from his wife, Irina, which contained the photograph. It is clear his problem is how to react to this new knowledge which has plunged him into emotional confusion.

The Beginning section could be said to end with the sentence: That was the way he'd used to read Solzhenitsyn.

Middle

Here, we learn the motivation for Arkady's subsequent struggles to solve his problem – to make his decision. We also see the tension beginning to build as, inexorably, the emotional screw starts to turn.

- He feels ashamed at the warm tone of the letter.
- Irina reminds him of days past in Timoshenko Park.
- She mentions her boss, Mr. Beritkhov.
- She says she wishes he would come back for the New Year. (At this point, a hint of mystery is introduced: why hadn't their mutual friend brought the letter, personally?)
- Irina says she may have to leave her flat and that Mr. Beritkhov has offered to find one just for her. (Here, the stranger sits down beside him and speaks in Russian, adding to the suspense.)
  (Note how the situation is worsening for Arkady)
- The stranger tells him he could return home, if he wishes, promising he would become a major soloist in the Conservatoire. He reminds Arkady of Russians' love of

music, their willingness to queue in the cold for hours in order to hear it, in contrast to the West.

- Arkady, in his mind's eye, pictures Irina in Mr. Beritkhov's arms and his son forced into an inferior school.
- He sees a poster advertising his performance, now peeling in the rain and revealing last week's celebrity beneath. Next week, he realises, his own name will be obliterated – and asks: but what about love?
- *The Climax* (this is the worst possible moment of the story). He sees a woman and a small boy; he is dark-skinned and clutching a puppet, just like his son in the photograph. For a second, Arkady thinks it could be them and calls out to them to wait. The woman turns and, just in time, snatches the boy from the jaws of the traffic. Arkady freezes in horror.

Ending

- In his imagination, the woman and child had become his wife and son – tragedy had been so close.
- The envelope is now lying in the road, wet and begrimed, but the letter is still in his hand – the important thing.
- As he turns to go back to his hotel, he has made his decision.

There is no need to dot the i's and cross the t's: the understatement produces a more powerful effect. The letter and photograph, his love of Russia, his feelings of homesickness have won. We know he intends to return home.

The theme – what the story is about:
its implied 'message'

This becomes obvious as the story progresses: Home is where the heart is. It is encapsulated in the title and its premise is proved by the ending so that the reader or listener feels completely satisfied. And the Main Character, Arkady, has learned a valuable lesson, too. Love is more important than fame and even than supposed freedom: his roots are still deep in his homeland.

Unities

- Unity of Time: the story takes place within a couple of hours at most, from its opening to its ending. (Flashbacks do not break the Unity.)
- Unity of Place: it all takes place entirely in Vienna.
- Unity of Action: it is told entirely from Arkady's viewpoint.

This illustrates, perfectly, how observance of the three Unities results in tight construction and a successful short story.

You can use the above analysis as a guide to the structure and composition of others, either published or your own. As has already been said, there is time enough for breaking the 'rules', for experimentation, once you have proved that you know what you are doing.

Descriptions

These are painted in with a light hand and add to the emotional quality of the story, being an integral part of it, not merely embellishments. They are the to be desired deft 'brush-strokes'.

- Russian sunsets
- Wheatfields
- Birch trees
- Timoshenko Park in autumn
- The stranger's eyes, golden like a carp's.

The practical side
of writing

WORKING METHOD

Those just starting to write are often inordinately interested in the working methods of established writers. It's as if
they think there might be some magic key that will open the
door of success, if someone will only tell them where to find
it. This is not a completely erroneous assumption. There is,
indeed, a key (or, more correctly, a password) which will
unlock the door and allow you into the hall of, if not fame,
then at least some degree of success. The word is: work.

Numerous writers have uttered statements on this subject, all of which come down to much the same thing.

James Michener: 'I know so many people who want to be
writers. But let me tell you, they really don't want to be
writers. They want to *have been* writers. They wish they had
a book in print. They don't want to go through the work of
getting the damn book out. There is a huge difference.'

Henry Miller: 'When you can't create, work.'

William Faulkner: 'I only write when I feel like it – and I
feel like it every morning.'

Sinclair Lewis, in a talk to university students on the
problems of the literary craft: 'One man works best in a
desert and the next in a jazz rehearsal room. One before
breakfast and one after midnight.' He continued: 'There is

only one fixed rule for writing and that is hard and unpopular. The story that you have not set down in words will never win glory, no matter how many evenings you have spent in delighting yourself and annoying your relatives by relating its plot. Which is an elaborate way of saying . . . work!'

Agatha Christie, in *An Autobiography*, said that the moment she changed from an amateur to a professional was when ' . . . I assumed the burden of a profession, which is to write even when you don't want to, don't much like what you are writing and aren't writing particularly well.'

And here's Mark Twain, in answer to a remark about his 'good luck': 'Yes, and the harder I work, the luckier I get.'

There is also a well-known saying that writing is five per cent inspiration and 95 per cent perspiration. I think that says it all. Only by constant practice do we master any craft – and writing is no exception.

None the less, many famous writers tell of gimmicks, rituals they need to observe in order to get down to their daily stint. Hemingway told of having to sharpen six pencils each morning before he could start. Steinbeck, in *Journal of a Novel*, tells how he began each day by writing a letter to his friend and literary agent before getting on with his novel. Some feel they can only write in school exercise books or on certain sized paper. Others have to write in longhand while others are able to create directly on to a typewriter or wordprocessor. But these are only idiosyncratic devices to help get their creative juices flowing. In the end, it still means getting down to the hard slog of work.

Time

We've all heard that cry of some would-be writers: I'd love to write if only I had the time! Arnold Bennet once said: 'We all have exactly the same amount of time – 24 hours a day.' As with anything else, it is a question of choice. However filled your life is with other pursuits, only *you* can decide on your priorities. It may not be easy to set aside an hour or two (or even half an hour) each day but everyone can manage that much time, *if they want to enough*.

Think-time Long before any writer begins putting 'black on white', he will have been thinking about his story, his characters, how he sees the plot unfolding. In that same lecture previously referred to, Sinclair Lewis affirmed: 'Most of the work of writing a novel is done in the author's mind before he makes a mark on paper – though after that he must have the patience to make such marks, eight hours a day for a year or so.'

Hemingway always finished his daily stint at a point where ' . . . you still have your juice and know what will happen next and you stop and try to live through until the next day when you hit it again.' Many other writers find this method helps shorten the 'warm-up' process when they start work again.

Self-discipline There can be few writers who would not admit to willingly doing anything to put off getting down to their writing, each day. The sun's shining after a long spell of rain so they ought to just mow the lawn, do the washing, clean the windows. If they don't pop down to the shops, right now, the bakers might sell out of brown bread – and so on and so on.

Along with the need to deal with the siren voice that lures you away from your desk, typewriter, wordprocessor or pen and pad, is the need to respect your talent and insist that others respect it, also. It is all too easy to allow others (especially if you're a woman) to distract you by assuming that your writing isn't all that important. If it is to you, then make sure others realise that.

Remember that we all have choices. If you want time to write, then be firm about letting your family and friends know this. If at all possible, set aside a regular time when you will not be available to them. Get up half an hour earlier each morning. Give up watching TV for an hour each evening. Make yourself a notice that states WRITER AT WORK – DO NOT DISTURB and hang it on the door of your chosen workplace. You have as much right to time and space for yourself as anyone else. Keep reminding yourself of that.

Writer's block

If you have never experienced writer's block, then thank your lucky stars. This is the awful phenomenon that can occur part way through a novel (usually at about chapter three or four) when one's imagination seems to have dried up completely. Most writers, at some point in their career, know only too well how devastating such a period can be – their book won't seem to 'move'. It is probably the reason why so many novels are abandoned.

If this happens, the truly professional writer will ask himself, first of all – is the whole idea and plot of the book, in fact, workable? If the answer is 'yes', then he has sufficient experience to be able to put it aside. If the answer is 'no', then he has to find a way to deal with the block. Various ways have been espoused by numerous writers, some of which are given below:

- Put your novel aside for a while and try something else (maybe a short story) so that you come back to it fresh.
- Do something physical for a few hours, like walking or gardening.
- Force yourself to keep on writing anything at all, even if it has no real connection, in the hope that, eventually, you will get the story moving again. (I've tried this approach myself, and it only resulted in deepening my depression and frustration and so it is not one I, personally, would recommend, but it does work for some.)
- Stop working on your novel and spend a few days nourishing yourself. Give yourself time to daydream, commune with nature, read some of those books you never seem to have got round to, before. Reading in the same genre might well spark off some fresh ideas that will get you going again. You won't be stealing because there is no copyright in ideas. You will merely be putting a little more water into the well of your imagination as you see how another writer has managed those twists and turns of plot that have kept his or her story moving.

Finally, if it happens to you once, perhaps you could put it down to experience. If it happens to you twice, however, to quote Lady Bracknell in *The Importance of Being Earnest*, it rather 'looks like carelessness'. In that case, I suggest you take Phyllis Whitney's advice (in *Guide to Fiction Writing*) and, with your next novel, start planning in detail by keeping a notebook into which you put every tiny idea for plot, characters, setting and so on as they occur to you. (See Section Two for more details.)

MECHANICS OF WRITING

Whether or not you compose in longhand, when it comes to sending work out to an editor or publisher, it *must* be typed. Therefore, it makes sense to teach yourself to type, if you can't already (or you can always use the two-finger method employed by many writers and journalists). And buy yourself a typewriter, manual or electric (a decent second-hand one will suffice, if you can't afford a new one). Otherwise, you will have to pay or persuade someone to type your work for you. There is another very good reason, though, for doing it yourself, even if only in the revision stage. There is no doubt that it is much easier to see the faults and weaknesses in your story, and to correct them, if it is type-written in double-spacing.

Today, of course, more and more writers are using word-processors so this seems an appropriate place to discuss them. Without doubt, they can reduce the amount of time spent on revising those first drafts. At the touch of a key, a word can be changed, the position of a sentence or paragraph altered, thus eliminating all those crossings out and re-typing needed with the old method. You can also print out as many copies as you wish, so no more carbons or photocopying will be necessary. Wordprocessors are also much less noisy than typewriters, so you can work late or early without disturbing anyone. Just leave the printing out until next day, as printers themselves can be noisy!

For those who are contemplating purchasing one, there are good models on the market at prices varying from a few hundred pounds to thousands. Before you make your decision, try to talk to writers who use one. Take into account the running costs involved as well as the initial outlay. For instance, a daisy-wheel printer produces better 'copy' but is more expensive to use, while a dot-matrix is no longer the anathema to publishers it once was, provided ribbons are well-inked and the high-quality printing facility is used.

Finally, however, you should never lose sight of the fact that no machine, even the most sophisticated, can create by itself. It cannot make you into a better writer. Only you have the power to do that – by hard work and perseverance.

Revision

It is a rare author who can produce a successful work at first go: most need several drafts before they consider it sufficiently polished to submit to an editor or publisher. Some hone their words again and again in the pursuance of excellence:

'I rise at first light and I start by rereading and editing everything I have written to the point I left off. That way I go through a book I'm writing several hundred times.' Ernest Hemingway.

'I revise the manuscript till I can't read it any longer, then I get somebody to type it. Then I revise the typing. Then it's retyped again. Then there's the third typing, which is the final one. Nothing should then remain that offends the eye.' Robert Graves.

Re-writing and editing is every bit as important as the first, more creative part of writing. After you are satisfied that what you have written is as good as you can make it, put it away for a few weeks, if possible, then take a critical look at it again. You may be surprised to find you can improve it even further before you send it off to a publisher or editor, at last, thus increasing its chances of success.

You may well find there are repetitions that need to be edited out (usually, given some thought, it is possible to find a synonym or to omit a word or phrase entirely without the meaning becoming ambiguous). Perhaps you've been too liberal with adjectives or adverbs. Some of the phraseology

Specimen page of revised draft

~~enclosed spaces out~~ *was a very open space* in ~~the~~ desert ⌊where she would, ~~literally,~~ have Philippe

breathing down her neck, ~~super-charging her pulse, panicking her into~~ *Yet her pulse-rate quickened*

~~another ignominious attack of claustophobia.~~ *just the same*

He gave a brisk nod.

'Very well. If you're ready, then. Khassim and Fatima will meet us

with the car at Saqqara to drive us home and someone from the stables will

ride the horses back.

Philippe ~~looked coolly competent~~ *was*, clad in cream jodphurs that

emphasised the lean hardness of his thighs, gleaming leather boots and

white open-necked shirt ~~from which rose the bronzed pillar of his neck. He~~ *with*

~~also had~~ a sweater tied loosely around his waist, ~~and had suggested Matlin~~

~~did the same.~~ 'It can be quite cold, riding across the desert sands at

night,' he'd warned and ~~she~~ had ~~taken his advice~~. *Matlin followed suit* Not having proper

riding gear, though, she'd had to make do with jeans and canvas shoes and

hoped they would prove adequate.

~~To show him she hadn't changed her mind,~~ *As* Matlin slid her foot into the

stirrup and ~~vaulted lightly~~ *swung herself* into the saddle, Philippe followed suit and, *side by side*

~~seconds later,~~ they ~~were~~ clatter*ed*ing out of the stable-yard, ~~Philippe~~

~~slightly ahead, leading the way.~~

'~~We will~~ *Take* it slowly, at first,' he ~~called over his shoulder~~ *said*.

'Later, ~~we will let them~~ *they can* have their head.'

Matlin nodded ~~her agreement~~, hiding her apprehension as ~~she felt~~ the

power-house of sinew and muscle beneath her strain*ed*ing to be released. She

prayed that, once she gave the signal, she could control the animal. But, ~~as~~

stet as a cool breeze caressed her cheeks and she settled into the steady rhythm

of the mare's trot, ~~her spirits~~ *she* began to s~~piral upwards~~ *relax*.

Overhead, clusters of stars studded the dark canopy of the sky, ⌈like

fistfuls of rhinestones ~~tossed there by some unseen giant,~~ and a topaz moon may seem clumsy, on re-reading, or some of the dialogue not ring true.

Before the advent of the wordprocessor (which many writers now use), it was possible to see a single page of text re-written or re-typed several times in draft form to illustrate the necessity of revision. Now, however, a word, a phrase, a sentence, a paragraph can be rubbed out at the touch of a key – like magic. Wonderful. But future generations will no longer be able to marvel at the crossings out and alterations to the MSS of our masterpieces. They will just have to take our word for it that we haven't worked any less hard at our stories; that we have revised as carefully as ever any writer did in a less technical age. A word of warning, here: because of the ease with which it is possible to tap out your ideas, beware of allowing self-indulgence to creep into your writing through not editing firmly enough.

But, if any one thing distinguishes the amateur from the professional, it is the willingness to re-write. And, if you want to join the ranks of the latter, accept and embrace this fact.

PRESENTATION

The way in which a manuscript (MS) is presented to an editor or publisher can make the difference between acceptance and rejection simply because it can affect its chances of receiving more than a cursory glance. After all, editors are human and, if they find a MS is hand-written or typed with a worn ribbon so that they have to strain their eyes to read it or with words running off the edge of the page, their initial reaction is bound to be negative.

Recently, I heard a well-known literary agent bemoan the fact, too, that lowered standards of literacy have become more noticeable over the past 10 years. He said he saw examples of this in the 50-odd MSS that arrived on his desk each week, frequently containing spelling and grammatical mistakes. His personal pet hates, he confessed, were bad punctuation and dialogue wrongly set out.

If those first few pages of your MS indicate a complete lack of professionalism, is it likely anyone is going to read on with any enthusiasm? After all, if the author thinks so little of what he has written that he hasn't considered it worth while to take the extra time and trouble to submit it correctly and to eliminate those errors, why should not an editor or agent treat it with the same lack of consideration?

When it comes to the way in which you make corrections to your MS, there is no problem if you are using a word-processor. If you use a typewriter, you may be lucky enough to have one with an erase key, or it is permissible to white out (with one of the proprietary products on the market) provided there aren't too many of them on the page so that it looks messy. In that case, better by far to retype that page.

To ensure that your story or novel is not rejected out of hand the moment it is taken out of its envelope, the following rules should be observed:

- Check for spelling and grammatical errors.
- Type in double-spacing (*not* single or even 1½) on one side only of A4 paper and leave a generous margin all round – minimum of 1in (2.5cm).
- Number pages consecutively. Chapters should *not* be numbered separately.
- Make sure dialogue is correctly set out.
- Don't use a worn ribbon.
- On a cover-sheet, state the title of the piece submitted, its length (to the nearest 100 words for a short piece and nearest 1,000 words for a full-length work), pseudonym (if used), your name, address and telephone number, rights offered and date.
- Keep a copy for your own file in case the original is lost.
- Enclose a stamped self-addressed envelope or, in the case of a full-length work, stamps to cover possible return postage. It is also useful to include a stamped addressed postcard for acknowledgement of its safe receipt (in fact, most publishers, and the BBC, automatically acknowledge receipt but few magazines do so).
- Keep any covering letter brief and to the point.

Specimen cover sheet

```
                      THE RETURN


                         by


                   AGATHA SMYTHE


                                    \




A short story submitted by:

Ms Angela Smith,
14 Rowan Street,
MERRITON,
DH15 3BN

Telephone. 0059 405312




Approximate length: 3,500 words


First British Serial Rights




11 January 1991
```

- Never enclose pages of MS in a binder of any kind: editors hate them. Place a full-length MS in an empty typing-paper box (secured with an elastic band) or in a reinforced envelope.
- Never turn up in person at a publisher's offices (except to hand in your MS at reception).
- Never telephone to enquire about your MS. If you haven't heard anything after two months, write a brief, tactful enquiry letter.

COMMON GRAMMATICAL ERRORS

We all seem to have our little blind spots when it comes to grammar, and a skilled copy editor will be on the look-out for these. That does not mean, however, that we don't have to be on guard against them ourselves – far from it! So here are some pointers to help anyone in need.

Possessive pronouns   is an area where grammatical mistakes frequently occur, with apostrophes being incorrectly added. The following should clarify their use:

ITS (often confused with IT'S which is a contraction of IT IS and, therefore, not a possessive pronoun)
OURS   YOURS   THEIRS   WHOSE
Possessive pronouns (or PP), as the name suggests, denote possession: thus: It's (it is) my contention that the business world does not know its (PP) arm from its elbow. Who's (who is) to say whose (PP) statement that is.

The plural of collective nouns   is also often written incorrectly when indicating possession. The apostrophe should come *before* the 's', as shown:
MEN'S   WOMEN'S   CHILDREN'S   PEOPLE'S
But: Companies' (plural) secretaries should hang their coats here while this company's (singular) secretaries should hang their coats there.
The noun 'people' can itself, of course, be used in the plural when it indicates more than one group of people, eg:

the peoples of the world. NONE is singular, not plural: it means, NOT ONE. Therefore: None of these books *is* of any use. (Not one of these books is of any use.)

Certain nouns and verbs are often confused; for example, advice and advise; licence and license; effect and affect.

I would advise (verb) you never to give unsolicited advice (noun).

If you wish to license (verb) the use of your premises for sale of alcohol you must apply to the authorities for a licence (noun).

The effect (noun) of reading this book, hopefully, will affect (verb) your writing skills.

Turning a noun into an adverb nearly always means losing a letter. For example: Humour becomes humorously. Skill becomes skilfully.

Single, double or hyphenated? Some words (which, in fact, are two or even three) are often, incorrectly, written as one – or hyphenated.

All right (not alright).

Dare say (not daresay).

If in doubt about any word, *always* check it out in a dictionary.

Punctuation Because punctuation is a complex subject, if you are unsure about it, use a good grammar book to guide you.

Spellings If you are in the least uncertain, check with a dictionary. It's amazingly easy to slip up. A lot of people have difficulty over deciding whether or not some words contain a double letter, such as: accommodate. Or whether words end in 'able' or 'ible', as in respectable and compatible. Two words that have caught me out, in the past, to my intense chagrin, are: proffer and implacable.

Over 100 Alternatives to 'Said'

Snapped	Protested	Rejoined
Screamed	Exhorted	Remarked
Yelled	Complained	Suggested
Bellowed	Exclaimed	Directed
Stormed	Railed	Informed
Snarled	Rebuked	Appealed
Screeched	Chivvied	Answered
Shrieked	Retorted	Announced
Grizzled	Declared	Countered
Hissed	Cried	Enquired
Sneered	Wept	Flashed
Exploded	Howled	Began
Sniped	Moaned	Continued
Roared	Sighed	Comforted
Shouted	Gasped	Blurted
Taunted	Sobbed	Intoned
Jeered	Mumbled	Interrupted
Mocked	Babbled	Advised
Jibed	Wheezed	Stammered
Snorted	Drawled	Stuttered
Tormented	Purred	Coaxed
Hollered	Whispered	Boasted
Raged	Rejoined	Bragged
Spat	Quipped	Inferred
Grunted	Giggled	Vowed
Groaned	Joked	Insisted
Sulked	Prattled	Called
Chided	Sniggered	Quoted
Begged	Burbled	Replied
Prayed	Chortled	Asked
Soothed	Gushed	Stated
Interrupted	Teased	Confided
Grumbled	Laughed	Carolled
Spluttered	Persisted	Breathed
Opined	Pontificated	Lied
Hinted	Expounded	Offered
Demanded	Explained	Insinuated
Expostulated	Added	Queried
Asserted	Enthused	Wailed
Commanded	Expanded	Maintained

DEALING WITH REJECTION

Rejection is a very emotive word. It is hard to keep in mind that it is only a piece of writing that has been rejected, when it comes winging back, and not ourselves.

However difficult it may be, try to see it in a positive light. To have got as far as completing an article, short story or novel, to have revised and polished it until it is as good as you believe you can possibly make it, and then to have submitted it to the critical eyes of a publisher or editor, is progress. Whatever results from that, it is a not inconsiderable landmark in your budding career.

If it is returned with either a rejection slip or a polite 'thanks but no thanks' letter, once you've swallowed your disappointment, read it through, again, as objectively as you can. You may see some glaring faults that you can correct before sending it out, once more.

This is where perseverance comes in – and determination. Perseverance is, indeed, a function of success and, if you want to succeed, you *must* persevere. Accept rejections as an inevitable, albeit painful, part of learning your craft because, almost always, you can learn something from them. And if an editor has gone to the trouble of telling you *why* your story has been rejected, take it as a sign s/he considers you have potential. You could even re-write it, in the light of those remarks, and re-submit it with a short, covering letter of explanation. In any case, it would do no harm to write and thank the editor for his/her comments.

To give you support and encouragement during such difficult periods, it helps to have sympathetic friends around you: people who *understand*. The best place to find them is in a writers' group. There are nearly 400 writers' circles around the country, with many local authorities running creative writing classes, also. While it is perfectly possible to learn to write alone in your own home, the comradeship of others of like-mind is invaluable.

Success is important for our self-confidence. I have seen the change in many students after they've received just one acceptance. As Somerset Maugham in *The Summing Up* said: 'It (success) can only give him (the writer) two good things:

one, the more important by far, is the freedom to follow his own bent, and the other is confidence in himself.'

LITERARY AGENTS

A literary agent is someone who sells a writer's work for him or her, negotiating a contract and getting the best possible terms. An agent also often advises on changes s/he believes will improve the chances of a MS being published.

It often seems to struggling writers like a *Catch 22* situation because, until they have had a book accepted, they usually can't get an agent and they feel they can't get a book published unless they have an agent. Like everyone else, however, agents are in business to make a living and, therefore, can only afford to take on an author whom they think will be successful, if not immediately then eventually.

It is also a very personal relationship and works best if author and agent are compatible and trust each other.

In return for his or her efforts, an agent charges a fee which is usually a minimum of 10 per cent of monies earned by the work in question. One or two reputable agents are now requesting a reading or handling fee, although most still do not.

When approaching an agent, always send a preliminary letter, giving brief biographical details, listing your successes to-date (if any), stating your aims and ambitions and giving a short outline of your book (a couple of paragraphs is sufficient). Then ask if s/he would be willing to look at your book and take you on. It is both polite and politic to include a stamped, addressed envelope.

EPILOGUE/SUMMING UP

My last piece of advice is an exhortation: take heart and persevere. Every time you complete a short story or a novel, give yourself a mental pat on the back. You've proved you have the staying power to finish a piece of writing. Reaching the point where you send something out to an editor or publisher is an achievement in itself, even if it comes winging back with a rejection slip attached. It means you have taken yet another step on the road to becoming a writer. Courageously, you've put your writing to the test and sent your 'baby' out into the cold commercial world.

Continue to nourish yourself as a writer by observing everything and everyone around you, by living creatively. And when you start to despair at ever finding success and feel like giving up, remember Aristotle's remark: 'The life so short, the craft so long to learn.'

Finally, have courage and never forget the three Ps – Practice, Polish and Perseverance. They will pay dividends, in the end.

In brief

NET BOOK AGREEMENT (NBA)

Controversy continues to rage (and doubtless will long after publication of this book) on the fairness or otherwise of the Net Book Agreement. This is a decades-old agreement between publishers and booksellers that no book shall be sold for less than the price shown on the cover. (This does not apply to those sold by Book Clubs, for which special rights are negotiated.)

If the NBA disappears, almost certainly, it will mean that books will become, even more than they are now, mere commodities. They will probably be on sale at large discounts in supermarkets, next to soap-powder or sausages, as well as in bona fide book shops. Unfortunately, that might result in the demise of many of the small booksellers who wouldn't be able to buy in sufficient bulk in order to compete with their new rivals.

The main worry for writers is whether or not such an eventuality would decrease even further their chances of having their work accepted.

MINIMUM TERMS AGREEMENT (MTA)

The Society of Authors and The Writers' Guild, jointly, drew up a standard contract containing terms which they considered were fair and reasonable to an author. After years of campaigning, the agreement to accept this was signed by a small number of leading publishers, beginning in 1978. Today, more and more are following suit. This is not to say that those publishers who have not accepted the MTA are in any way disreputable but, for those authors without an agent, it provides a useful guide to ensure they are getting a fair deal.

A copy of the MTA is obtainable from The Society of Authors, price £1 plus a s.a.e. (See *Useful Addresses* on page 132.)

PUBLIC LENDING RIGHTS (PLR)

Once you have a book published (fiction or non-fiction and even, surprisingly, if it has been vanity-published), provided it has an International Standard Book Number (ISBN) – see later entry – it is eligible for registration with the Public Lending Rights Office and, thus, for receiving monies from the PLR fund.

This fund was set up by the government as the result of long and vigorous campaigning by the Society of Authors, The Writers' Guild and a number of well-known authors. Its aim is to redress, to some extent, the previously-existing iniquitous situation in which writers received no extra monies for their work no matter how many times their books were taken out from public libraries. It works like this: a sample number of libraries is used (this list changes annually and, currently, consists of 30, with only 16 in 1983, the first year of operation) and the number of times any one book is borrowed is recorded. These figures are multiplied by the number of libraries around the country to give a representative number of borrowings per book.

For the past few years, the amount distributed has remained at around £3 million. The sum paid to authors is just under 1½p per borrowing with an upper limit of £6000 per annum per author, the majority (around 11,000) receiving less than £100. This provides for the average author, who rarely makes a livelihood out of writing alone, a small but obviously welcome addition to income.

Further details of the scheme can be obtained from: The PLR Office. (See *Useful Addresses.*)

CONTRACT

Once your book has been accepted, you will receive a formal contract from the publisher. This will contain a number of clauses and will be signed by both publisher and author. It is wise to go through the entire contract very carefully so that you know exactly what you are signing. That is where obtaining a copy of the Minimum Terms Agreement from The Society of Authors would be helpful (or joining the Society). On pages 125 and 126 we include part of a contract supplied by The Society of Authors.

ADVANCE

This is the sum of money, agreed between author and publisher and stated in the contract, which is paid in advance of accrued royalties. It invariably applies to non-fiction, but it is rare for a first-time novelist to receive an advance.

It is normal practice for it to be paid in three parts: the first on signing of the contract, the second on receipt by the publisher of the completed MS and the third upon publication.

ROYALTIES

These are always stated in the author's contract and are in percentage terms of the book's published price. Normally, and depending on the type of book, they will be 7½ per cent

MEMORANDUM OF AGREEMENT made this

between

hereinafter called the PROPRIETOR (which expression shall be deemed to include the PROPRIETOR's Executors, Administrators and assigns) of the one part and

hereinafter called the PUBLISHERS (which expression shall be deemed to include the PUBLISHERS' permitted assigns in business and any other subsidiary or associate of

of the other part, concerning a literary work at present entitled

(hereinafter called the Work) of which the author

(hereinafter called the Author)

whereby it is mutually agreed as follows:

Rights

1. The copyright in the Work shall remain the property of the PROPRIETOR. The PROPRIETOR hereby grants to the PUBLISHERS the rights

    (a) to produce and publish and sell the Work either as a whole or in part in volume form in the English language; *and*

    (b) to sub-license the volume rights and subsidiary rights in the Work hereinafter specified.

Territories

2. The rights granted to the PUBLISHERS under Clause 1 hereof shall be sole and exclusive throughout the world.

Duration

3. (a) The rights granted under Clause 1 hereof shall subsist for a period of 20 years from the date of first publication of the Work by the PUBLISHERS (hereinafter called the initial term)

    (b) On every tenth anniversary of the date of first publication of the Work by the PUBLISHERS (or within a reasonable time thereafter) either party hereto may give written notice to the other that such party wishes specified terms of this Agreement relating to royalties or subsidiary rights to be reviewed, in which case such terms shall be considered in the light of comparable terms then prevailing in the publishing trade and shall be altered (with effect from the date of such notice) to the extent that may be just and equitable. Failing agreement on what may be just and equitable the matter shall be referred to arbitration under Clause 25 hereof

    (c) If the Work shall be in print (as hereinafter defined) at the end of 17 years from the date of first publication of the Work by the PUBLISHERS, the PUBLISHERS may inform the PROPRIETOR in writing of the date that this Agreement is due to expire and invite the PROPRIETOR to negotiate in good faith with the intention of reaching agreement on revised terms for a further period. The PROPRIETOR, if so requested by the PUBLISHERS, shall inform the PUBLISHERS of the terms offered (if any) by other publishers and the PUBLISHERS shall be given the opportunity to offer equal terms and should the PUBLISHERS do so then the PROPRIETOR shall accept the PUBLISHERS' offer unless in the PROPRIETOR's view mutual trust and confidence between the parties hereto shall have broken down

(d) If, with the PROPRIETOR's consent (such consent not to be unreasonably withheld), a sub-licence is granted by the PUBLISHERS extending beyond the initial term, any reversion of rights to the PROPRIETOR hereunder shall be without prejudice to the continuation of such sub-licence and the PUBLISHERS' entitlement to their share of the proceeds therefrom. However, the PUBLISHERS shall not be entitled to extend or renew, without the PROPRIETOR's consent, any sub-licence granted which is due to terminate after the initial term (unless and until a further agreement shall be reached under (c) above).

Delivery of typescript

4. (a) The PROPRIETOR shall arrange for 2 legible copies of the complete typescript of the Work to be delivered to the PUBLISHERS in accordance with the specifications included in Appendix 1 hereto. Such typescript shall be professionally competent and shall be ready for the *typesetter*. If the typescript of the Work in final form shall not have been delivered to the PUBLISHERS by the date specified in Appendix 1 hereto the PUBLISHERS may agree with the PROPRIETOR a later date for delivery or may give the PROPRIETOR reasonable notice in writing to deliver such typescript. If the PROPRIETOR shall fail to deliver such typescript by such agreed date or within such notice period then upon request from the PUBLISHERS the PROPRIETOR shall repay to the PUBLISHERS any and all monies theretofore paid to the PROPRIETOR hereunder and this Agreement shall thereupon terminate and all rights hereunder shall revert to the PROPRIETOR

(b) Within 30 days of receipt of the typescript of the Work by the PUBLISHERS the PUBLISHERS shall notify the PROPRIETOR if any alterations to the typescript of the Work will be required or if such typescript is to be rejected. Within a further period of 30 days (or such reasonably necessary longer period as may be notified to the PROPRIETOR) the PUBLISHERS shall specify the required alterations or provide detailed reasons, in writing, for rejection. Should such typescript be rejected by reason of the PROPRIETOR's failure to comply with the Clause and Appendix 1 hereto then upon request from the PUBLISHERS the PROPRIETOR shall repay to the PUBLISHERS any and all monies theretofore paid to the PROPRIETOR hereunder and this Agreement shall thereupon terminate and all rights hereunder shall revert to the PROPRIETOR. The PUBLISHERS shall take all reasonable care of the typescript of the Work, but shall not be responsible for loss thereof or damage thereto while in the PUBLISHERS' possession or in the course of production or in transit.

or 10 per cent for the first UK and Commonwealth edition. They are usually paid twice-yearly *after* the author's advance against royalties has been earned.

FIRST BRITISH SERIAL RIGHTS (FBSR)

Whether in full or initials only, this should be stated on the cover sheet of an article or short story. In effect, it means you are offering a newspaper or magazine the right to print your piece for this first time only. In other words, you are retaining your copyright. (Should you omit this by mistake, by implication, that is still what you are offering – not your copyright.) If, at a later date, you think you might be able to sell it again, you can only offer Second British Serial Rights. You should then inform the next editor where and when it has previously appeared.

Although it is unusual to be able to sell second rights, it is just possible, under certain circumstances (for example, in a widely-different circulation area), that another editor might be interested. However, this is not to say that you cannot use the *facts* in an article and totally re-write it for a different readership and with another slant.

LIBEL

If an author, in his writing, has caused an identifiable living person to be held up to hatred, ridicule or contempt, he could be sued for libel in a court action. It is wise, therefore, to be absolutely sure that none of your characters can be even remotely connected with anyone alive. The dead cannot be libelled.

A copy of The Society of Authors' *Quick Guide to Libel* can be obtained from them, price £1 (free for members).

PLAGIARISM

This is perhaps the worst accusation that can be made against any author. In effect, it means stealing someone else's work. While, as we've already discovered, there are no new plots under the sun (and so, to some extent, it is impossible not to steal one), none the less, it behoves every writer to ensure his own storyline bears no close resemblance to that of any other.

COPYRIGHT

A complex law (updated with effect from 1989) governs this but, in essence, it means that whatever anyone writes (be it a novel or a letter) *the actual words written* belong to him or her alone and they cannot be reprinted without his/her permission or that of his/her heirs. This copyright remains effective until 50 years *after his/her death* (not, as is sometimes erroneously believed, 50 years after it was published).

Another misconception is that it is necessary to add the symbol (C) to your MS, declaring it to be your copyright. It might look attractive but it is entirely superfluous: you have written it and that is sufficient to make it legally yours.

Note: Copyright laws in the United States are somewhat different to those in the UK. Check with your publisher or with The Society of Authors.

MULTIPLE SUBMISSION

This is the term used to describe a MS that is sent out to more than one publisher at the same time. It is still considered a controversial practice in the UK and rather frowned upon but is becoming widely accepted in the US.

BLURB

This is the brief résumé of the storyline of a novel, or description of a non-fiction book, which appears on the book's cover. Its intention is to entice a potential reader to purchase it. If you are lucky enough to have your book published, the blurb is *not* something you need be concerned with. It is almost always written by the editor.

HYPE

This is a word often bandied about in connection with best-selling fiction which is frequently said to be 'hyped'. Basically, it means that a book will be vigorously promoted by the publishers through a big advertising campaign in the media, through the author's appearance on TV chat-shows, radio programmes and touring the country for book-signing sessions. Originating in the US publishing world, it is a shortened form of 'hyperbole', meaning to exaggerate or blow up beyond the truth. Thus, sometimes, a book can become more successful than it deserves to be.

REMAINDER

Books, like perishable commodities, have an expected shelf life. Once that date has passed, publishers usually 're-mainder' unsold copies to companies specialising in buying and selling them. These are the heavily-discounted books you find in cut-price book shops and this arrangement does not countermand the NBA. An author's contract should offer him the opportunity of buying his own books at a substantially reduced price, if this unfortunate situation arises.

VANITY PUBLISHING/SUBSIDY PUBLISHING

These are virtually one and the same thing. The use of the word 'vanity' says it all. Any author, unable to find a bona fide publisher to accept his work and who then pays to see it in print is, in effect, pandering to his own vanity. It is well to remember that reputable publishers *never* advertise for authors so beware of any firms that do. The financial cost is always high and rewards likely to be negligible because few retailers will stock such books – and it may be a very long time before it is even actually printed. Nor is it likely they will earn PLR because libraries, generally, will not buy them either.

SELF-PUBLISHING

This method of publishing is growing in popularity now that desk-top publishing is increasing and is not the same as vanity publishing. It involves the author in the entire process, from writing through to selling. It is, however, expensive as well as time-consuming and is not to be recommended without careful thought, expert advice and determination. Some authors, however, have found it to be a successful way of publishing and selling their work.

BOOK PACKAGING

This is a growing phenomenon in the book world, particularly in the world of heavily illustrated non-fiction. Some companies, known as book packagers, either originate or buy a MS outright (that is, the author relinquishes his copyright), then they put together the entire package of MS, illustrations (if required) and printing and offer it to a publisher for sale under the latter's imprint. Although this means the author will not usually receive any royalties, the sum offered him should reflect those anticipated.

INTERNATIONAL STANDARD BOOK NUMBER (ISBN)

This is the 10-digit number found on the cover of all books published since 1970. It is normally arranged by the publisher and is necessary in order for it to be eligible for PLR.

FACTION

This is a fairly new word which has come into being to describe a piece of writing which is a blend of fiction and fact. Dramatised documentaries could be said to come within this category.

COMPETITIONS

There are now many writing competitions held annually which are open to anyone in the country (and even attracting overseas entries). There are also those run by magazines, both as a means of promoting sales and finding new contributors, and by writers' circles to boost funds. It is up to the individual to look out for announcements of these in the press, libraries and bookshops. They provide a useful deadline which is often a spur to getting down to writing.

Always study the rules of each one, carefully, and abide by them. Invariably, they will insist on entries being typed in double-spacing and state a maximum number of words – don't exceed this or you risk disqualification. Some will also have a set theme. Obviously, stories which win a magazine competition will be those considered suitable for that particular publication so it behoves you to study several issues before attempting to enter.

A few of those held annually are:

BBC – Radio Drama (details in Radio Times)
Mobil Oil – Drama
The Mail on Sunday – Opening of a Novel

The Ian St James Award (Short Story by writer who has never had a book of fiction published)
Bridport (Dorset) – Short Story and Poetry (most libraries have details)
Stand Magazine – Short Story
The Sunday Times – Travel Article
Woman's Own – Short Story
Swanage (Dorset) Arts Festival Literary Competition (Short Story and Poetry)

Writers' magazines usually carry details of most competitions. Also most writers' circles will receive information from various sources (which is another reason for belonging to one).

USEFUL ADDRESSES

The Society of Authors,
84 Drayton Gardens,
London SW10 9SB

The Writers' Guild of Great Britain,
430 Edgware Road,
London W2 1EH

The Society of Women Writers & Journalists,
Hon. Secretary, Mary Witt,
1 Oakwood Park Road,
Southgate,
London N14 6QB
(Probationary members accepted)

The Romantic Novelists' Association,
Contact:
Marina Oliver,
Half Hidden, West Lane,
Bledlow,
Nr Princes Risborough,
Buckinghamshire HP17 9PF

PEN (Poets, Essayists, Novelists),
21 Earls Court Square,
London SW5 9DE

The Book Trust,
Book House,
45 East Hill,
London SW18 2QZ

The PLR Office,
Bayheath House,
Prince Regent Street,
Stockton-on-Tees,
Cleveland TS18 1DF

The Arvon Foundation (writing courses),
Totleigh Barton,
Sheepwash,
Devon EX21 5NS
(Also at Lumb Bank, Heptonstall,
Hebden Bridge, W. Yorkshire
HX7 6DF)

Writers' Summer School
(annually, mid-August at The
Hayes Conference Centre,
Swanwick, Derbyshire – early
application necessary)
Hon Sec. Philippa Boland,
The Red House,
Mardens Hill,
Crowborough,
Sussex TN6 1XN

Writers' Holiday (annually, South
Wales, mid-July)

Administrator, Anne Hobbs,
30 Pant Road,
Newport,
Gwent

Creating Writing Holidays in
France
(organised by Leicester Study
Groups)
LSG,
201 Main Street,
Thornton,
Leicestershire LE6 1AH

USEFUL PUBLICATIONS

An Authors' Handbook by David Bolt (Piatkus 1986)
Directory of Writers' Circles, compiled by Jill Dick, available from Oldacre,
  Hordens Park Road, Chapel-en-le-Frith, Derbyshire SK12 6SY
Dictionary of Quotations (Penguin)
Easily Into Desk Top Publishing by Peter & Joanna Gosling (Macmillan
  1991)
Freelance Market News, Cumberland House, Lissadel Street, Salford,
  Manchester M6 6GG (monthly)
Freelance Writing and Photography, Tregeraint House, Zennor, St Ives,
  Cornwall TR26 3DE (quarterly)
Fowler's Dictionary of Modern English Usage (OUP 1965)
Guide to Fiction Writing by Phyllis Whitney (Poplar Press 1984)
Guide to Literary Prizes Grants & Awards in Britain and Ireland available from
  The Book Trust, Book House, 45 East Hill, London SW18 2QZ
How to Write for Children by Tessa Krailing (Allison & Busby 1988)
Quartos magazine (for competitions), BCM-Writer, London WC1N 3XX
  (bi-monthly)
Quick Guide to Libel (Society of Authors 1987)
Research For Writers by Ann Hoffman (A & C Black 1986)
Roget's Thesaurus (Longmans 1962 – Penguin edition)
Romantic Times and Fiction Writers' Monthly, 163 Joralemon Street,
  Brooklyn Heights, New York 11201, USA
Thirty-Six Dramatic Situations by Georges Polti (The Writer Inc, USA
  1977)
The Writer's Handbook (Macmillan/PEN – annual)
Writers' and Artists' Yearbook (A & C Black – annual)
Writing Historical Fiction by Rhona Martin (A & C Black 1988)
Writers' Monthly, 18/20 High Road, London N22 6DN
Writers' News, Subscriptions: Stonehart Subscription Services, Hainault
  Road, Little Heath, Romford RM6 5NP (monthly)

The Writer, 120 Boylston Street, Boston, MA 02116, USA (monthly)
Writer's Digest, 9933 Alliance Road, Cincinnati, OH 45242, USA (monthly)
(The above two American magazines, and *Thirty-Six Dramatic Situations*, are also available from: Freelance Press Services, Cumberland House, Lissadel Street, Salford, Manchester M6 6GG